Collins

Cambridge International
AS & A Level
Global Perspectives
and Research

WORKBOOK

Series editor: Mike Gould
Authors: Mike Gould, Lucinda Misiewicz and Lucy Norris

William Collins' dream of knowledge for all began with the publication of his first book in 1819. A self-educated mill worker, he not only enriched millions of lives, but also founded a flourishing publishing house. Today, staying true to this spirit, Collins books are packed with inspiration, innovation and practical expertise. They place you at the centre of a world of possibility and give you exactly what you need to explore it.

Collins. Freedom to teach.

Published by Collins
An imprint of HarperCollins*Publishers*
The News Building
1 London Bridge Street
London
SE1 9GF

HarperCollins*Publishers*
1st Floor, Watermarque Building, Ringsend Road, Dublin 4, Ireland

Browse the complete Collins catalogue at
www.collins.co.uk

British Library Cataloguing-in-Publication Data
A catalogue record for this publication is available from the British Library.

Authors: Mike Gould, Lucinda Misiewicz and Lucy Norris
Series editor: Mike Gould
Publisher: Elaine Higgleton
Product managers: Lucy Cooper and Sundus Pasha
Product developer: Natasha Paul
Content editor: Tina Pietron
Development editor: Judith Walters
Proofreaders: Sonya Newland and Catherine Dakin
Cover designer: Gordon MacGilp
Internal designer and illustrator: Ken Vail Graphic Design Ltd
Typesetter: Ken Vail Graphic Design Ltd
Permissions researcher: Rachel Thorne
Production controller: Lyndsey Rogers
Printed and bound in the UK using 100% Renewable Electricity at CPI Group (UK) Ltd

Third-party websites and resources referred to in this publication have not been endorsed by Cambridge Assessment International Education.

Cambridge International recommends that teachers consider using a range of teaching and learning resources in preparing learners for assessment, based on their own professional judgement of their students' needs.

The publishers gratefully acknowledge the permission granted to reproduce the copyright material in this book. Every effort has been made to trace copyright holders and to obtain their permission for the use of copyright material. The publishers will gladly receive any information enabling them to rectify any error or omission at the first opportunity.

An extract in 1.4 from "Singapore eco-tourism plan sparks squawks of protest" by Sam Reeves, AFP, 09/01/2019, http://doc.afp.com/1BL4Z5, copyright © Agence France-Presse, 2019. Reproduced by permission of the publisher.

The publishers would like to thank Dean Roberts for reviewing a sample of the Workbook in development.

MIX
Paper from
responsible sources
FSC C007454

This book is produced from independently certified FSC™ paper to ensure responsible forest management.

For more information visit: **www.harpercollins.co.uk/green**

Contents

Introduction

About the syllabus

Unlike other syllabuses, Cambridge International AS & A Level Global Perspectives and Research (9239) is predominantly skills-based. It allows you to explore your own interests, whether in the future of artificial intelligence, in global inequalities, or in the causes and management of global pandemics.

Cambridge Global Perspectives™ encourages the development of high-order skills such as analysis, problem-solving and critical thinking, as well as research, collaboration, communication and reflection. These skills are relevant and highly transferable to other subjects of study and to the world beyond.

> *Information in chapters 5–11 in this book is based on Cambridge International AS & A Level Global Perspectives and Research (9239) syllabus. However, all the advice and guidance is written by the authors of this book. References to assessment and assessment preparation are the publisher's interpretation of the syllabus requirements and may not fully reflect the approach of Cambridge Assessment International Education. You should always refer to the appropriate syllabus document for the year of your examination to confirm the details and for more information. The syllabus document is available on the Cambridge International website at www.cambridgeinternational.org.*
>
> *Registered Cambridge International Schools benefit from high-quality programmes, assessments and a wide range of support so that teachers can effectively deliver Cambridge qualifications.*
>
> *Visit https://schoolsupporthub.cambridgeinternational.org to find out more.*

The Workbook

This Workbook complements the Student's Book and offers space for development of practical skills, such as note-taking, planning, mind-mapping and self-evaluation. As you work your way through the course, this Workbook will help you to keep track of your progress and record your journey in a journal-style format. This allows you to develop a personal working portfolio, assists you in planning and timekeeping and encourages self-reflection.

How to use this book

The Workbook is split into two parts:

Part 1: Supporting your work and skills

Chapters 1–11 will give you further practice in the Cambridge International AS & A Level Global Perspectives and Research syllabus. Each unit is covered in one double-page spread to give you a structured approach.

Each unit starts with a brief introductory text to outline the objective of the unit, to show you what it covers and why it's important to the overall course.

A number of activities will help you to develop your work and build on the practical skills you have learned in the Student's Book. There are a variety of new sources and extracts in the Workbook. These have all been written by the authors as exemplars.

The key terms and language support box offers guidance and support for language, particularly in writing academic English.

The reflection box prompts self-reflection and provides you with ideas that you could include in your reflective log (the journal or notes you use to track your ideas, choices and thoughts about your work).

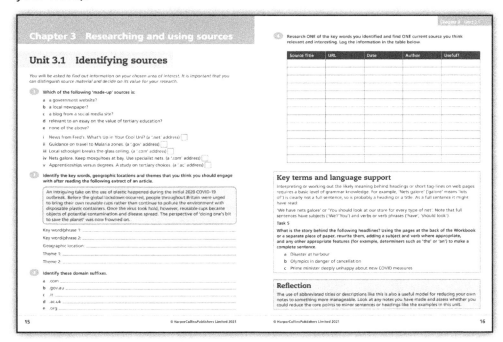

Part 2: Tracking your work and progress

Part 2 consists of four sections that provide you with pointers and guidance to use as a journal and track your progress. Topics covered are aligned with the four components: the written exam, the Essay, the Team Project and the Research Project. Each section includes useful tables, diagrams and enough space to write into.

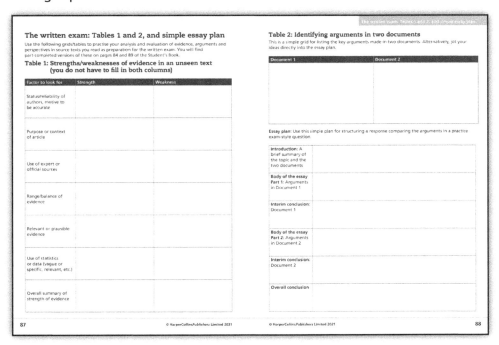

Unit 1.1   Becoming a global thinker

To get the most out of the Cambridge International AS & A Level Global Perspectives and Research syllabus, you need to consider your own position within it and what you will get from it.

1   **Here are several possible reasons why you might have chosen this course, or why it might suit you. Add one or two of your own, if they are not mentioned here, and then rank them in terms of importance to you (1 being low, 10 being very important).**

Reason	Rank (1–10)
I think I will get a good grade in it.	
It will widen my knowledge of global issues.	
I will be able to link it to subjects I enjoy studying.	
I like the chance to collaborate and work with others.	
It gives me the chance to work independently, pursuing my own interests.	
It is a core component of the AICE Diploma.	
It will help build my general English skills.	
I think it will help my job prospects.	
It covers lots of different skills, such as how to analyse.	
My additional reason 1	
My additional reason 2	

2   **Imagine you needed to apply for this course by writing a letter. Write 50–75 words, using the pages at the back of the Workbook or a separate piece of paper, explaining why you think this is the course for you, and what you aim to get from it.**

3   **As a way of encouraging the 'global thinker' in you, look at the topical issues on the next page from current and recent times. Choose two or three issues and spend five minutes jotting down everything you know about each one, using these five questions:**

What do I think about this?

Where have I heard about this?

Where does my thinking and knowledge come from?

Does everyone think like this? Why/why not?

How would I find out more information about this?

Issues

The rights of transgender people

Choosing whether or not to have a vaccination for an infectious disease

Private (paid for) education

Colonising planets

Limiting air travel

Genetic modification for food provision

Key terms and language support

When describing learning styles or attributes, we often use words with useful prefixes to distinguish between similar ideas or meanings – for example, _inter_personal in which _inter_ means 'between'.

Someone who works well in a team has good _interpersonal_ skills (good 'between people' skills).

Task 4

Look up the prefixes in the words below and use them to work out what each phrase means. Do they have positive or negative connotations?

intrapersonal skills   _interdependent group members_

anti-social behaviour   _student who is extrovert or introvert_

Reflection

Think about yourself as a learner again. How has your knowledge of the syllabus changed between first hearing about it and completing this unit? What were the key factors that helped you gain knowledge and understanding of it?

Unit 1.2 Topics, issues and themes

It is important that you have a secure knowledge of the key vocabulary required. Much of this will crop up, but you need to know some core terminology from the start.

1 **The box below includes a number of terms and statements related to a global topic.**

> People's country of birth should be the main factor in identifying race or self
>
> Rights of transgender people   Identity politics has created a 'me-first' generation
>
> People identifying as transgender should have free access to gender realignment surgery
>
> Changing identities   Racial profiling or categorisation

Using the pages at the back of the Workbook or a separate piece of paper, identify:

a the global topic that is common to all of these

b the issues that are narrower, more defined aspects of the topic

c the points of view on these issues.

2 **Complete the following diagram, which explores a different topic to show how themes can lead you onto issues.**

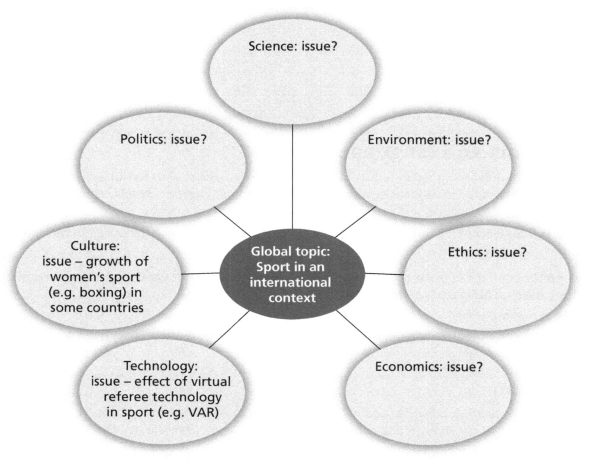

Science: issue?

Politics: issue?

Environment: issue?

Culture: issue – growth of women's sport (e.g. boxing) in some countries

Global topic: Sport in an international context

Ethics: issue?

Technology: issue – effect of virtual referee technology in sport (e.g. VAR)

Economics: issue?

Key terms and language support

The best thing you can do to increase your academic English is to actively 'notice' aspects of language structures, spellings and words that are used together. Complete this quiz about the list of Global topics on page 6 and Themes on page 9 of the Student's Book, which is designed to help you notice and grow 'language detective' skills!

Task 3

a • Are the capitals in these lists always used to refer to these terms? Search online and find examples where they are used in the middle, not just the beginning of sentences.

_____

  • When *must* capitals be used in English as a general rule?

_____

  • How is this the same as or different from other languages you use?

_____

b Can you correctly identify the parts of speech of all these words – i.e. are they nouns, adjectives, etc.?

_____

c Can you find an example of two adjectives used together? If you reverse the order, does the meaning change?

_____

d Can you find examples of one adjective and two nouns? Does the adjective describe both?

_____

Reflection

Think about and log the skills you have covered in Unit 1.2 of the Student's Book. Answer the reflective questions below.

• Which ideas (e.g. *topics, issues, themes*) and skills (e.g. *collaborative mind-map making, searching online with others*) were new to you?

• Which would you like to research or discover more about? Why?

• Did anything stop you from learning in class/independently during this unit? If so, what?

• How will you help yourself/get support to catch up?

Unit 1.3   What is the Critical Path?

The Critical Path is central to your study of Cambridge Global Perspectives, but integrating the language around it and its practice can be challenging.

 1 A student has begun to make notes about an issue they are considering researching. Match each of the questions raised to one (or more) aspects of the Critical Path (deconstruction, reconstruction, reflection, communication and collaboration).

Global topic	Sport in a global context
Theme/Issue	Technology/use of technology to enhance performance
Potential question	Does new technology give an unfair advantage to some athletes?
Source material	Article in *The Guardian* reporting on World Athletics' President Sebastian Coe's comments on Nike's running shoes
	https://www.theguardian.com/sport/2021/jan/03/sebastian-coe-nike-spikes-athletics
	Accessed 23/06/21

	DEC	REC	REF	COM&COLL
a What are my initial views on the use of advanced technology to enhance sports performance?	☐	☐	☐	☐
b What views (other than Coe's) are there on the fairness/unfairness of using advanced tech?	☐	☐	☐	☐
c What is the key vocabulary around sports technology that I will need to define and refer to in my writing?	☐	☐	☐	☐
d How could I draw on the knowledge of others – perhaps in my class or school – to progress this research?	☐	☐	☐	☐
e Are other brands giving advantages to athletes? Can I synthesise the scientific evidence for various brands or sports?	☐	☐	☐	☐
f Have I changed my views at all in the light of this article?	☐	☐	☐	☐
g What is Coe's view of Nike's running shoes? Where is this evidence coming from?	☐	☐	☐	☐

> **Key:**
> DEC = deconstruction
> REC = reconstruction
> REF = reflection
> COM&COLL = communication and collaboration

Key terms and language support

Language for academic use: *It is important to consider the forms of new words to prepare for paraphrasing.*

It is important to identify the word class for a key term from the course and consider additional word classes linked to the term you could adopt when paraphrasing. Being able to express an idea differently, and paraphrase key points as you read and make notes are core academic skills. It helps you to avoid too many direct quotations both in note-making and in your essay writing, but where ideas are taken from key sources you will still need to cite or acknowledge these.

Task 2

Choose four new words from the unit and complete the table below. Note that not all words can be changed to fit every word class.

Noun	Verb	Adjective/opposite and prefixes	Adverb
communication	to communicate with someone (communicated)	communicative *un*communicative	(un)communicatively
analysis	to analyse something/someone (analysed)	analytical *over*-analytical	analytically
investigation	to investigate something/someone		
(self-) awareness	to be aware of something/someone	aware *un*aware	
judgement	to judge something/ someone	judgemental* ('judgy')* *negative idea*	judgementally

Reflection

Log the skills you have covered in Unit 1.3 of the Student's Book by answering the reflective questions below.

- Which aspects of the Critical Path do you need to research or discover more about? Why?
- What helped you to learn in class/independently during this unit?
- How will you start to record and learn new words (e.g. using a grid or table like the one above)?

Unit 1.4 Exploring the Critical Path approach to topics, themes and issues

Being able to summarise and synthesise parts of texts or other sources is an important skill to master for successful deconstruction and reconstruction. Often, this starts with basic comprehension.

 1 **Read the following extract from the article on page 16 of the Student's Book.**

> But the project in the Mandai district has ruffled the feathers of environmentalists. They believe that rather than promote biodiversity, it is too imposing for the area, will destroy forest habitats and they say insufficient safeguards were put in place before work began – leading to animals being killed on roads.
>
> The row has highlighted concerns about rapid development in space-starved Singapore, and worries that some of the country's more wild and green corners are being lost only to be replaced with something more artificial.
>
> 'I think you are getting your priorities wrong if you are replacing natural heritage with captive breeding,' Subaraj Rajathurai, a veteran wildlife consultant, told AFP.

Circle the letter of the statement below that best sums up the text. Think about which of them covers the overall issue, the perspective/point of view and the key detail.

a Singapore is struggling to find space for green areas and natural habitats.

b Industrial development such as the Mandai one is causing huge problems in a country that values its green spaces.

c Environmentalists are not convinced that current development projects such as the Mandai one are encouraging biodiversity.

d Lack of security in development projects like the Mandai one has led to a lot of road-kill.

Key terms and language support

Language for academic use: *reading and paraphrasing*

Each of the statements in Task 1 paraphrases the article. How can you do this yourself?

Read and reread a whole text several times to make sure you understand it. Make notes of the key points only *after* you have understood the text.

- Do *not* underline or highlight the words you don't know! Instead, consider highlighting or underlining everything you understand. Look at the gaps and see if you can work out what is being expressed anyway. If not, decide if that is important overall. Only research or look up a word if you think it is very important.

- You might find it useful to highlight or underline key sections and ideas or main points. You will need to paraphrase these, which will help you summarise (and avoid 'copying' texts).

- Handwrite your key points and notes, and come back to them later. This will help you expand words into your own form. Do not forget to reference your sources as you go, to save you trying to find them again afterwards. Make a physical or computer-based folder or file of your original sources. You can scan or photograph any paper texts.

Paraphrasing tips:

- Use synonyms (words that have the same or similar meanings); *change the words* in the text and/or *reorder the ideas*, but don't copy!
- Select a different starting point in the key sentence(s) you want to rephrase. This will help you to *change the structure*.
- By changing the *form* of a word, you will change the structure of the sentence.

Task 2

Look at these examples and match the strategies with the tips above. Has the meaning changed?

a While it may be best known as a financial hub with scores of high-rise buildings, tropical Singapore is…

Singapore, a centre of international finance, is widely known for its…

Strategy:_____

b Now jungle is being cleared to create a green tourism hub it is hoped will eventually attract millions of visitors a year.

An ethical tourist hub is being built on land cleared from jungle, with the aim of

increasing the numbers of international visitors by the million.

Strategy:_____

c For example, the continued expansion of ecotourism has created opportunities for income generation and employment at both the national and local levels.

Nationally and locally, both employment and the generation of income have been

boosted by the on-going growth of ethical tourism.

Strategy:_____

Reflection

Think about and log the skills you have covered in Unit 1.4 of the Student's Book. Answer the reflective questions below.

- What new skills did you develop or practise over the course of this unit? How will they help your life and language skills, and your academic learning?
- What questions do you have? Look at the work you have produced and the notes you have made. Identify areas or skills you need more help with.

Unit 2.1   Analysing arguments

It is important to understand some of the basic features and aspects that make up arguments.

1 **Circle the letter(s) of the following that are assertions (claims made without support or reasoning).**

   a   If we want people to continue climbing Everest, then we need to reduce human waste on the routes.

   b   Everest is the most polluted mountain on the planet.

   c   Pollution can be found everywhere; recent ice melts have even revealed it on our highest mountain.

   d   There are many global problems, but reducing pollution is each nation's number one priority.

2 **Each of these arguments represents a particular type of idea: a generalisation, a causation and a correlation. Write 'GEN', 'CAU' or 'CORR' next to each one.**

   a   Successful students in the Humanities tend to be those who read widely in their youth.

   b   The teenager I interviewed did not own a mobile phone, which shows that it's a myth that teens are dominated by their attraction to social media.

   c   The presence of election monitors ensured that people were able to cast votes freely and without fear.

3 **The following extract from an article demonstrates the use of counter-arguments.**

> Whilst it might be argued that enforcing lockdown in a pandemic causes substantial mental suffering, the alternative is clearly worse: the uncontrolled spread of a virus that causes severe infection and is often fatal. Others oppose lockdown on different grounds, believing that 'herd immunity' or 'population immunity', predicated on the notion that allowing the virus to spread naturally eventually leads to a decline in the virus through having insufficient bodies to infect. However, organisations such as the WHO (World Health Organization) have comprehensively dismissed this idea and suggested that such immunity can only be achieved by vaccination and coherent global approaches, such as lockdown, to controlling the spread.

   a   What is the main argument being proposed here?

   _____

   _____

   b   Underline the two counter-arguments that the writer acknowledges but then disproves or objects to.

c Here is a further counter-argument to using lockdown as a way of controlling a pandemic.

Lockdown infringes basic human rights and liberties.

Write a further sentence or two acknowledging this counter-argument but arguing against this idea. You could begin:

Although some people...

Key terms and language support

Modals are used to express ideas such as possibility, ability (to do something), intention, certainty, suggestion, obligation, etc.

Writers often use a range of modal forms in texts to subtly alter the tone or impact of a point of view. For example: _Some might argue that lockdown infringes human rights..._

Here, the use of the modal 'might' suggests possibility. This phrasing would be very useful if you were arguing in favour of lockdown in emergencies, as it acknowledges the other view but weakens it by using 'might'. You can change the impact, making the counter-argument stronger, by removing the words 'might' and 'some': _People argue that..._

Task 4

In the following interview, identify the modal forms and how they are being used. Make a note of how weak or strong they are.

Reporter: You must admit it's a very serious situation.

Scientist: It could be argued it is no more serious than it was at the start of the pandemic.

Reporter: Really? You should see the queues outside our local hospital.

Scientist: Well, that may be the case, but there could be a number of reasons for that.

Reporter: So, you're not concerned?

Scientist: No. I will check out the data, but I'm sure it is not as bad as you think.

Reflection

Find any opinion piece and evaluate your own understanding of arguments by identifying the key argument, any examples of causation, correlation or generalisation and, if present, any use of counter-arguments.

Unit 2.2 Understanding perspectives

The syllabus definition of a perspective is 'a coherent world view which is a response to an issue. A perspective is made up of argument, evidence and assumptions and may be influenced by a particular context'. So, they are made up of several aspects.

1 **The examples in the table are elements of an expressed perspective. Read each example and decide which aspect from the box below applies to which example. Write the aspect in the table.**

Example	Aspect
Restricting online work to work hours reduces stress in the workplace.	
An 'always-on' culture means that employees can never escape the workplace, meaning that the divisions between home and work are blurred, which is damaging.	
Professor Alicia Lopez of…is a researcher who seeks to understand company policies and business practices. She states that a reduction in the use of work email at home may lead to less stressed employees and thus more productivity in the longer term.	
Stress in the workplace.	
Lopez works for an independent think-tank, which conducted research amongst employees at the top 50 large companies listed on the stock market index in the USA.	

Aspects to add to the table:

> Issue Assumption Argument Evidence Context

2 **Can you think of at least two alternative perspectives on the same issue? You could consider:**

- geographical context
- personal/cultural context (consider who was surveyed in the examples above)
- political context
- scientific context
- ethical context

a Another perspective could be that of _____

_____

b Another perspective could be that of _____

_____

3 **The following article from the CEO of a business introduces a perspective that challenges the one expressed in the table.**

I hear a lot of criticism of the 'always-on' culture by commentators outside the business environment, yet few of these critics actually know how businesses run or understand the pressures on them to be as efficient as possible. The argument that the stress induced by being available as an employee '24/7' is outweighed by the evidence within my own business. When my employees were offered the opportunity to have an 'email-off' structure from 7 p.m. to 8 a.m., they universally rejected the offer and preferred to retain the current system. They cited the opportunity it gave them to catch up on correspondence they'd been unable to do during office hours, and also wanted to show clients their willingness to 'go the extra mile'. It also gives me the chance to check in regularly with my managers, say, and keep abreast of changes in the business. In addition, we operate globally: our usual working hours here are 'home' hours on the other side of the world. What message would we send if we were unavailable to our business partners in China just because we'd all left the office?

a   In what way does this perspective challenge or contrast with the one expressed in the table?

   The writer claims that...

b   Using the pages at the back of the Workbook or a separate piece of paper, identify at least one argument the CEO mentions to support this perspective.

c   In what ways could the evidence or support presented here be regarded as unreliable or create a narrow perspective?

Key terms and language support

In defining perspectives, you will use a number of adjectives that are synonyms of 'different', such as 'contrasting', 'opposing', 'alternative', 'competing', 'conflicting'.

Task 4

On a scale of 'difference', where would you place each of the synonyms listed above? You may need to check the meanings first.

Weakest		Difference		Strongest
1	2	3	4	5

Task 5

Think of any two arguments you have researched on the same topic. Answer the questions below, using the pages at the back of the Workbook or a separate piece of paper.

- How would you describe their perspectives?
- Why would you describe them this way?

Reflection

Think of an issue you personally feel strongly about. List at least two alternative perspectives (which may include ones you disagree with initially) on the issue. These need not be things you have read or sourced; they could be perspectives you imagine might exist on the issue.

Unit 2.3   Evaluating evidence

Being able to judge the quality or reliability of evidence is a core skill which you can learn and practise.

 The table below shows six examples of evidence related to the issue of workplace stress and its causes. Identify which of these is:

- primary evidence (P)
- secondary evidence (S)
- quantitative evidence (QT)
- qualitative evidence (QL)

Note that more than one category might apply to some examples.

Example	P, S, QT or QL
one hospital's records of numbers of people admitted with stress in 2020–21	
interview with employee of top law firm in which average hours worked per day is 16	
chart showing average working hours of employees in one country over 10-year time period	
television documentary called *Business Under Fire* featuring interviews with bosses of top firms about stress levels	
letter to employee from company admitting liability for stress-related illness	
research paper by science professor at medical school about changing levels of stress amongst workers during the COVID crisis	

 Read the extract on the next page from a text on the topic of vitamin deficiencies. How credible is this evidence, on a scale of 1 (not at all) to 10 (very/totally credible)?

Use one or more of these factors to decide:

- Does the source have a vested interest?
- What provenance does the publisher have?
- Is the evidence corroborated?
- Is the evidence provided by someone with the 'ability to see'?
- Is the evidence representative?
- Is the evidence credible?
- Is the evidence meaningful (does it have context)?
- Is the evidence relevant?

Questionnaires completed by patients who visited a selection of pharmacies along our eastern coastline revealed that over 80% trusted the advice given by pharmacists over the counter when it came to recommending a range of our vitamins for improving both physical and mental well-being. The same patients preferred our own brand over competing brands on a ratio of 6:1. They cited price point, packaging, ease of swallowing and clear instructions as drivers of their purchase. On this basis, we believe it is in the interests of your local council to roll out the supply of vitamins to all hospitals so that patients can have access to their preferred brand in 2021 – a brand that has been proven to reduce stress and anxiety.

Extract from marketing email by Marketing Director for BioSiGen Co, a pharmaceutical company that produces vitamins and medicines, to local health representatives

a On a scale of 1–10, the evidence is _____

b Write a brief paragraph explaining why you gave it this score.

I believe the evidence provided is... _____

_____

_____

Because... _____

_____

_____

Key terms and language support

It is important that in your own writing you can communicate your understanding using a range of phrases. For example, when evaluating evidence you might write that it 'shows/says that the issue is more widespread than initially thought'. However, there are a number of more academic expressions you could use, and it is also useful to look out for these in texts when looking for evidence. They are all slightly different in meaning.

The research signals that... indicates... demonstrates... proves... reveals... provides evidence that... suggests... tells us...

Task 3

Using the pages at the back of the Workbook or a separate piece of paper, rewrite this paragraph replacing the uses of 'shows'/'says'/'showed'.

The source describes research which shows how many people benefited from increased vitamin intake over 12 months. The tests used showed increased immune responses, which shows that vitamins may be beneficial in fighting common illnesses. The report says that clinicians could start prescribing vitamins as a matter of course from now on.

Reflection

If you were exploring the impact of vitamins on people's wellbeing, what credible sources would you seek out? Find at least two, and make a note in your log or journal about why these might be credible.

Unit 3.1   Identifying sources

You will be asked to find out information on your chosen area of interest. It is important that you can distinguish source material and decide on its value for your research.

1   **Which of the following 'made-up' sources is:**

   a a government website?

   b a local newspaper?

   c a blog from a social media site?

   d relevant to an essay on the value of tertiary education?

   e none of the above?

   i   News from Fred's. What's Up in Your Cool Uni? (a '.net' address) ☐

   ii Guidance on travel to Malaria zones. (a '.gov' address) ☐

   iii Local schoolgirl breaks the glass ceiling. (a '.com' address) ☐

   iv Nets galore. Keep mosquitoes at bay. Use specialist nets. (a '.com' address) ☐

   v Apprenticeships versus degrees. A study on tertiary choices. (a '.ac' address) ☐

2   **Identify the key words, geographic locations and themes that you think you should engage with after reading the following extract of an article.**

> An intriguing take on the use of plastic happened during the initial 2020 COVID-19 outbreak. Before the global lockdown occurred, people throughout Britain were urged to bring their own reusable cups rather than continue to pollute the environment with disposable plastic containers. Once the virus took hold, however, reusable cups became objects of potential contamination and disease spread. The perspective of 'doing one's bit to save the planet' was now frowned on.

Key word/phrase 1: _____

Key word/phrase 2: _____

Geographic location: _____

Theme 1: _____

Theme 2: _____

3   **Identify these domain suffixes.**

   a .com _____

   b .gov.au _____

   c .it _____

   d .ac.uk _____

   e .org _____

4 Research ONE of the key words you identified and find ONE current source you think relevant and interesting. Log the information in the table below.

Source Title	URL	Date	Author	Useful?

Key terms and language support

Interpreting or working out the likely meaning behind headings or short tag-lines on web pages requires a basic level of grammar knowledge. For example, 'Nets galore' ('galore' means 'lots of') is clearly not a full sentence, so is probably a heading or a title. As a full sentence it might have read:

'We have nets galore' or 'You should look at our store for every type of net'. Note that full sentences have subjects ('We'/'You') and verbs or verb phrases ('have', 'should look').

Task 5

What is the story behind the following headlines? Using the pages at the back of the Workbook or a separate piece of paper, rewrite them, adding a subject and verb where appropriate, and any other appropriate features (for example, determiners such as 'the' or 'an') to make a complete sentence.

   a Disaster at harbour

   b Olympics in danger of cancellation

   c Prime minister deeply unhappy about new COVID measures

Reflection

The use of abbreviated titles or descriptions like this is also a useful model for reducing your own notes to something more manageable. Look at any notes you have made and assess whether you could reduce the core points to minor sentences or headings like the examples in this unit.

Unit 3.2   Evaluating sources

Once you have found some sources, you need to work out how useful they are going to be for you.

1 What things would you look for to establish a potentially useful source?

_____

_____

_____

2 Define these terms from the RAVEN/CRAAP tests and say why they are important for you.

a Currency: _____

_____

_____

b Vested interest: _____

_____

_____

c Purpose: _____

_____

_____

d Ability to see: _____

_____

_____

3 List some warning signs you might come across in sources that would suggest they are not particularly reliable.

_____

_____

_____

_____

_____

4 What is your current view of the sources you have found? Write a few notes on each one summing up how reliable or not you think they are.

_____

_____

_____

_____

_____

Key terms and language support

When evaluating sources, you may not have time to read the whole source. It is important to check the provenance and credibility of the writer, but beyond that, there are several parts of a source that it is useful to look at to help you get a good sense of it without having to read the whole thing in detail.

Task 5

Match these terms to their definitions.

a Introduction	**i** A summative explanation usually on the back cover of a book, 'selling' its key idea or story.
b Blurb	**ii** A general term for the opening section of a report, speech, article or longer text, setting out some of the key ideas.
c Abstract	**iii** A set of chapter or section titles, usually numbered in the sequence they appear.
d Contents list	**iv** A reference section at the back of a longer text that allows readers to search for key words or terms, which are listed alongside the pages on which they appear.
e Index	**v** A summary paragraph at the start of an academic or scientific article or report, setting out the objectives and core findings.
f Conclusion/findings	**vi** A final section of a longer text, which draws together the key ideas or what has been found out.

Reflection

Test your own ability to make judgements about sources without reading the whole text by looking at each of the features listed in Task 4 where they exist. How much can you find out about the text from skim-reading these parts? Is there anything else you could add to the list of 'short cuts' for checking a text?

Unit 3.3   Using sources

You need to know how to use potential sources effectively. This means not simply copying information, but finding ways of explaining that information yourself, filling in the background and identifying evidence for your line of argument.

1   **How would you use the following information? The first has been done for you.**

Information	Use
a 76% of oysters in the United Kingdom have been affected by chemical pollution.	Factual evidence to support problem of chemical pollution.
b Plastic is a versatile substance that has become vital to humans.	
c Much plastic rubbish causes huge problems for river wildlife.	
d Trout are dying from ingestion of plastic bags, while water birds are being strangled by plastic rings from drinks bottles.	
e The government has legislated to ban single-use plastic bags.	
f Plastic does not biodegrade and is too often not recycled.	

2   **Select signal words from the word bank below for each of the following purposes:**

> acknowledge advise agree argue assert believe claim comment conclude
> concur confirm contend declare deny disagree dispute emphasise illustrate
> imply insist observe point out reject report respond suggest think

a   where you plan to use evidence from a source
illustrate, claim ...
_____

b   where you plan to set up a counter-argument
_____
_____

c   where you want to add support for a viewpoint
_____
_____

d   where your own viewpoint is being expressed
_____
_____

3 Using the statements of information from the table in Task 1 and some carefully selected signal words, write up a short, synthesised argument. The text has been started for you.

Plastic is a versatile substance that has become vital to humans. However, many would acknowledge that...

Key terms and language support

Paraphrasing usually involves rewriting in your own words. Part of this process may be about reducing the material you have read and then trying to find alternative words or phrases to express the same ideas.

Task 4

How has the source information below been paraphrased? Underline any synonyms used in the student's text and circle any information in the source text that the student has not included.

Source	Student
Since we reported on the planning phase for the new harbour development, we have seen an exponential rise in industrial outflows and spillage into the lagoon. Levels of tuna and red snapper, the two most fished varieties in the region, have diminished by 60% in the six months since construction began.	After the initial study, they described a huge increase in industrial pollution entering the lagoon. Quantities of popular fish in the area fell by 60% in the past six months.

Reflection

How do you try to improve the range of your vocabulary? Do you use the thesaurus function in your computer software, or do you use print thesauruses or dictionaries? Think of three ways you could improve the variety of words and phrases you use.

Unit 3.4   Academic style

It is important that you write in a way that communicates your thoughts, ideas and arguments coherently to a broad general audience. The register you use is the particular choice of language or structures you make – for example, how formal or informal it is – to match your audience or readers.

1 Write a sentence or two from each of the following, trying to match the register you use to the audience.

a An email to a friend explaining a topic of interest to you.

_____

_____

b An explanation to your teacher justifying why you want to explore a particular area.

_____

_____

c A formal argument that could be included in either an essay or a speech on a topic of interest.

_____

_____

2 Write an improved version of the passage below. Try to fix the following errors.

a 6 spelling errors

b 1 incorrectly used tense

c 5 lower cases that should be capital letters

d 2 word confusions

e 1 imprecise conjunction

f 1 example of redundancy

g 2 imprecise pronouns

h 3 generalisations

i 3 punctuation corrections

j 2 unreferenced facts

When can plastic not be a pollutant. This can be found in lots of countries wear excess to clean water was limited, despite to be one of key rites listed in the un declaration of human rights. It is seen in Zimbabwe, where waterbourn illness is pandemic families need to buy water in plastic botles to live the waste created is a large sauce of in come for some people to collect bottles to use showing a primary source of pollutants in the area being not plastic rather failed sewage systems. A final, last conclusion is that plastic is bad.

_____

_____

_____

_____

_____
_____
_____
_____
_____
_____
_____
_____
_____
_____
_____

Key terms and language support

Being clear about core terms in academic writing will help you to use them accurately and effectively.

Task 3

Write definitions of these key academic terms as a reference.

a Paragraphs: _____

b Topic sentences: _____

c PEAL/PEEL: _____

d Redundancy: _____

e Rhetorical questions: _____

f Finite verbs and participles: _____

Reflection

How good is your academic style at the moment? Give yourself a score on a scale of 1 (low) to 10 (high) based on the sorts of style and usage errors in Task 2. What steps could you take to improve?

Unit 3.5   Referencing

Referencing is a vital part of your essay, as it allows the reader to follow up on information and to confirm data.

1   **What is plagiarism? Write a short definition.**

_____

_____

_____

_____

2   **Which of the following sentences need references? Where in the sentence should the reference go and why?**

a   Research has shown that what the majority of Americans want is a country 'where they will not be judged by the color of their skin'.

_____

b   When arguing about the concept of school, it is important to remember that the origin of the word dates right back to the Greek concept of leisure, as only those with time could afford to study.

_____

c   68.5% of parents/guardians claimed they used the available feedback sheets at the end of school reports.

_____

d   I have been interested in the issue of plastic waste since the time I found a heron strangled with a milk carton ring.

_____

3   **When is the only time you can cut and paste information? Why?**

_____

_____

_____

_____

_____

Key terms and language support

When referring to reports, surveys or investigations you will probably need to indicate what the cited text shows.

Task 4

Work out what the underlined term means in each sentence, then write a brief definition.

a   The <u>findings</u> of the report were that Black people were disproportionately excluded from the most important roles in sporting organisations.

_____

_____

b   There were several <u>outcomes</u> of the enquiry, with the resignation of the Chair of the national basketball association being the most notable.

_____

_____

c   There were conflicting <u>results</u> from the survey: while 45% said they would be happy to favour positive discrimination, 30% said they thought there was already a level playing field.

_____

_____

d   The <u>implications</u> of the public enquiry were made very clear: if the government did not reform policy at the highest level, then the discrimination would continue for years to come.

_____

_____

Reflection

Check that you have used the same referencing system consistently across your work – for example, in terms of punctuation, the order in which references are listed or dated, and so on.

Unit 4.1   Working independently

Using graphic organisers will help your thinking processes in preparation for discussions and writing tasks, both in and out of class. You need the right one for the 'thinking job' you are asked to do.

1 **How can the visuals below help you process and organise your ideas? Match each one with the thinking (or cognitive) tasks a–f describe. There is more than one possible answer for each.**

    a Showing the causal links between events, arguments, ideas, i.e. cause and effect.

    b Recalling and summarising ideas and arguments.

    c Sequencing events, ordering ideas and arguments.

    d Decision-making, planning or reviewing ideas and arguments.

    e Deeper analysing: sorting, dissecting an idea or concept into separate, specific parts.

    f Synthesising ideas and arguments to reduce a body of information to its essence.
      For example: a = Bridge; Futures wheel; Fishbone chart

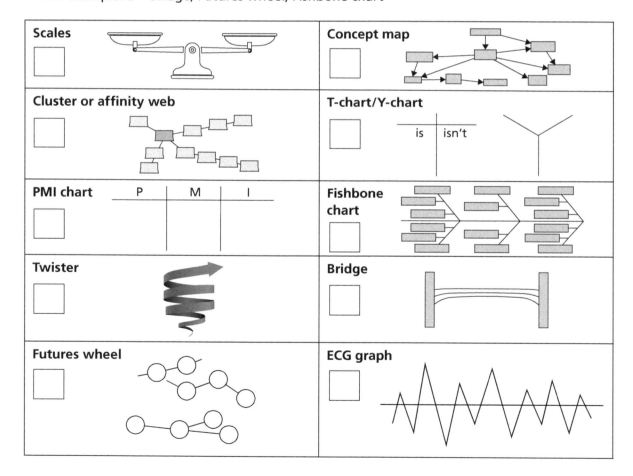

Scales ☐	Concept map ☐
Cluster or affinity web ☐	T-chart/Y-chart ☐ is | isn't
PMI chart ☐ P | M | I	Fishbone chart ☐
Twister ☐	Bridge ☐
Futures wheel ☐	ECG graph ☐

Cycle circle	Flow chart
☐	☐
Tri pie chart	**Funnel chart**
☐	☐

2 Look at the tasks set for this unit in the Student's Book, such as the Reflective plenary. Which organiser will help your thinking? Why?

_____

_____

_____

_____

_____

Key terms and language support

It is important to be as accurate and precise as possible when explaining charts, diagrams and other tabular forms. In particular, nouns related to change or relationships between data measures are important.

For example:

increase, rise, improvement, growth, decrease, fall, decline, worsening, reduction, drop

Look at any recent diagrammatic representation of data linked to an issue you are researching. Practise using these terms to describe what the data shows. Then consider how you could add appropriate adjectives to be even more precise, for example, 'rapid rise' or 'slight fall'.

Reflection

Choose a graphic organiser to make notes in as you answer these reflective questions.

- Which independent learning and study skills and tools were new to you?
- Which could you use to help you with home or independent study this week?

Use your answers to help you write an entry in your reflective log or journal.

Unit 4.2   Working in a team

Considering the benefits of shared group learning practices and strategies will help improve your study skills.

 Read and illustrate the texts below to show how the group learning strategies work.

Pitch to peer

This is when you take it in turns to sell or 'pitch' an idea for others to consider. The idea comes from a Hollywood 'elevator pitch' – or the time it takes to move between floors to interest a producer in making your film. Your peers listen, discuss and feed back or supply further thinking points.

For example:

Peer-review

This is when you review, assess or give feedback on each other's ideas or work. Often this will use success or other criteria to help structure comments.

Peer 'teach-back'

This is when you teach each other a concept, skill or idea you were taught in class when you need to review, check or develop your understanding. The idea is for you to share and improve your knowledge and skills in a non-judgemental way. If you miss a class, or find that you have some gaps in your understanding, you can ask a classmate to teach you. Teaching something to an individual or group also helps you check that you have understood something properly yourself.

---

2   **Match the purposes and benefits below to the strategies in Task 1.**

a   To push thinking further and consider different stances, viewpoints, perspectives.

_____

b   To reinforce what you have learned, to find out if you share the same understanding
as others.

_____

c   To help support improvement and supply ideas for completing work successfully.

_____

Key terms and language support

Creating a shared digital dictionary, particularly with classmates when you work on a project
together (like the Team Project), can be a great tool for recording academic language. It will
benefit your academic language knowledge and save time, if you collaborate on it with others.

• Decide what format and tools you will use to record writing, audio, images and links.

• How will you categorise the academic language? You could include subject-specific vocabulary
and general 'chunks', linking expressions, signposting phrases, and so on.

• A good dictionary entry will include different pieces of information, such as meaning
translations, useful grammar notes, pronunciation and examples.

• Look at this example entry.

> **to sign a treaty** – a formal agreement in law between groups of people or countries.
> Treaties are written down and signed by leaders of those countries involved.
>
> e.g. a _treaty_ was signed by First Nations Australians from both communities on
> 30 October 1872. Note grammar: often used in the passive, as in the example.

Task 3

**Write an example entry, using the pages at the back of the Workbook or a separate piece of
paper. Think about what else would help you (e.g. an image, a recording of the word being used
in the example).**

Reflection

Review the useful strategies for the most effective collaboration do's and don'ts (Student's Book
page 72). Use a visual organiser to help, for example:

Do	Don't
DO listen carefully when others are talking	DON'T assume that people are following what you say, and check by looking at their eyes!

Write an entry for your reflective log or journal, giving your reasons why these strategies are or
are not effective.

Unit 4.3 Developing reflection

Using appropriate language will help you to develop effective skills for reflection, in order to progress your learning.

1 **Look at the reflective thinking structures in a–d and expand them to make four meaningful sentences. For example: a** *Throughout our discussion, the team failed to focus on the task.*

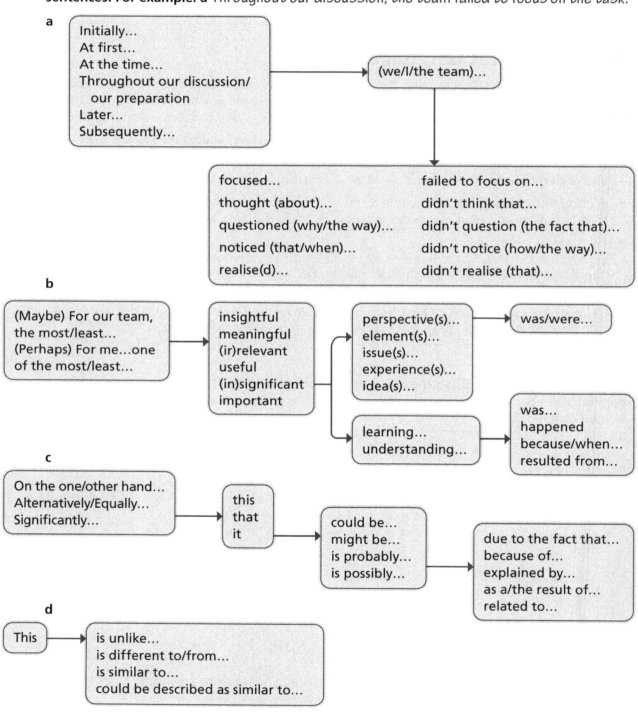

a

> Initially...
> At first...
> At the time...
> Throughout our discussion/
>   our preparation
> Later...
> Subsequently...

> (we/I/the team)...

> focused...   failed to focus on...
> thought (about)...   didn't think that...
> questioned (why/the way)...   didn't question (the fact that)...
> noticed (that/when)...   didn't notice (how/the way)...
> realise(d)...   didn't realise (that)...

b

> (Maybe) For our team,
> the most/least...
> (Perhaps) For me...one
> of the most/least...

> insightful
> meaningful
> (ir)relevant
> useful
> (in)significant
> important

> perspective(s)...
> element(s)...
> issue(s)...
> experience(s)...
> idea(s)...

> was/were...

> learning...
> understanding...

> was...
> happened
> because/when...
> resulted from...

c

> On the one/other hand...
> Alternatively/Equally...
> Significantly...

> this
> that
> it

> could be...
> might be...
> is probably...
> is possibly...

> due to the fact that...
> because of...
> explained by...
> as a/the result of...
> related to...

d

> This

> is unlike...
> is different to/from...
> is similar to...
> could be described as similar to...

a _____

_____

b _____

_____

c _____

_____

d _____

_____

2 **Label a–d in Task 1 with their key purpose, (A) analysis (I) interpretation or (E) evaluation.**

Key terms and language support

Task 3

Read what these students say about learning and practising new expressions. Which of the strategies do you use?

> *I record myself using new language expressions on the voice notes of my mobile phone. I pretend I am a lecturer or TV presenter, or that I am giving a talk. I can listen again and learn this way.* **Luca**

> *I use a notebook to create my own example sentences – but they have to be meaningful to me, I mean they have to relate to work or topics we are reading or learning about.* **Hiroki**

> *I used to copy the phrases down in a notebook 10 times. But my teacher explained that didn't involve any thinking! And it's true, it didn't help me. Now my friends and I challenge and test ourselves by making a shared multimedia digital dictionary. That super-charges my brain!* **Tom**

Look online for more ideas about how to learn and recall new expressions.

Reflection

Identify a recent learning experience to reflect on – for example, something you failed to learn or achieve and why. Make notes to answer these questions using the structures in Task 1.

- What happened or didn't happen? Why?
- What was challenging or difficult? Why?
- What do/don't you feel confident about? Why?
- What do you need to do another time?
- What will you try doing differently? Why?

Use your answers to write an entry for your reflective log or journal.

Chapter 5 Reading and responding to sources

Unit 5.1   Reading unseen sources

Establishing the gist of a text when you read it for the first time is an important part of the process of deconstruction and analysis.

1 **Which of these are most likely to help you establish the gist of an article? Tick all that apply.**

a the title and/or subtitle of the article ☐

b the name of the author ☐

c the topic sentences in each paragraph ☐

d repeated words or phrases ☐

e words or phrases linked to the same core topic ☐

f the number of words in an article ☐

g the author's background or job ☐

2 **Read this opening paragraph to an article.**

> Public health, private confidence
>
> *It is a responsibility of all health professionals and experts to promote the benefits of vaccines over any potential health risks. Vaccines for diseases such as smallpox, measles, cholera and tuberculosis, to name just a few, have all saved millions of lives and have had relatively few documented adverse impacts. In addition, whilst many would argue not having a vaccine is a personal choice, we have seen that asymptomatic carriers of a disease can pass on it on unsuspectingly to others, therefore vaccinating as many as possible is the only real way of establishing herd immunity, as it has popularly been called. But, those who have the knowledge about public health must speak up on behalf of vaccines as a key weapon against disease in a confident, well-informed way.*

a Underline the topic sentence in this article.

b List at least three key words or phrases that are repeated more than once in the text (ignoring words such as 'the' or 'and').

_____

_____

_____

c Highlight or circle any phrases or sentences that give a clear indication of the writer's viewpoint (this could be evidence for a point of view, for example).

d Make a note of anything significant about the writer of the article or her background.

_____

_____

_____

_____

3 **Write a sentence or two summing up what the gist of the article is likely to be from this opening paragraph.**

 The gist of the article is that _____

_____

_____

_____

_____

_____

Key terms and language support

You may have already come across the term 'semantic field' during the course. This is when a text contains a number of words and phrases that are broadly linked by topic or area. When exploring sources for the first time, the style and content of the text is often revealed by such 'fields'. For example, in the text in Task 2, words such as 'vaccine', 'disease', 'immunity', 'smallpox' and 'asymptomatic' could all be categorised under the heading 'disease'.

Semantic fields are not limited to vocabulary, but could also reveal grammatical usages – for example, related verbs or phrases ('inspected by…', 'under investigation', 'looked at in detail', etc).

Task 4

Take any of the sources you are currently using. Are any words, phrases or other grammatical usages linked in these ways? There may be several within one text. What do these 'fields' tell you about the text?

Reflection

In preparation for Unit 5.2, revise or review your understanding of the two reading skills, skimming and scanning. Which do you find easier to do? How can you practise or improve your skills in these key areas?

Unit 5.2   Identifying key points and issues

When you look for precise information in a text, you need to employ slightly different techniques from when you are trying to gain an overall understanding.

1   **If you were asked a question that needs you to find specific information in a text, or you were looking for a particular piece of information, how would you go about it? Tick any of the following techniques that apply.**

a   Scan the text for examples of the key words (or synonyms of them) from the information you began with.

b   Quickly skim-read the article from beginning to end, hoping to pick up the required information from the gist.

c   Check that the information you have found fits what you are looking for and isn't a 'false friend'.

d   Write out the whole sentence or paragraph that contains the right information.

2   **Explicit information is information that is stated clearly and obviously. Implicit information is information that has to be worked out, and which isn't stated so directly.**

Read this short extract from a blog.

> Imposter syndrome is the feeling people get that they do not deserve their success and that they might be 'found out' or revealed to be a fraud. For example, at least 65% of women running their own businesses said they suffered from 'imposter syndrome' according to a recent survey. I can vouch for that. Often, I have been overwhelmed by nerves when about to address a conference or lead a presentation, even on a topic in which I'm an expert.

Which of these sentences:

a   implies that the writer herself suffers from 'imposter syndrome'?

_____

_____

b   explicitly states that 'imposter syndrome' affects lots of women?

_____

_____

3   **Figurative language is often used to imply a point of view or a perspective.**

Here is more from the same blog by the same businesswoman.

> It is interesting that men do not suffer from imposter syndrome in the same way as women. Where women seem to feel vulnerable and wounded, men automatically erect a shield of invincibility and are always well-armed for battle.

a What is the metaphor used here to describe men's and women's confidence?

_____

_____

b What does it suggest about such men?

_____

_____

Key terms and language support

Identifying key information is easier if you understand the different parts of speech. These are shown in the table below.

Noun	Pronoun	Adjective	Determiner	Verb	Adverb	Preposition	Conjunction	Interjection
office	It	official	the, some, an, etc.	suggest	officially	after	so	wow, huh
fear	He/she/ they	fearful		be	often	under	and, or	

Why does this matter? If you are asked to find or identify information, sometimes it helps if you are looking for the same type of word or phrase. Equally, your understanding of a text may depend on you being able to work out the meaning of words due to their similarity (e.g. office, official, officially, etc). Finally, the function of words such as pronouns can help you track meaning – for example, understanding that 'it' may refer back to something previously mentioned. Such references back or forward in a text can be vital in following an argument.

Task 4

How many examples of each of these parts of speech (apart from interjection) can you identify in the extract about imposter syndrome? Create a table like the one above, using the pages at the back of the Workbook or a separate piece of paper, and add the words from the text to it.

Reflection

The verbs/phrases 'imply', 'infer', 'convey the idea that', 'hint at' and 'suggest' can all be used to state things less directly. Look again at the speech by John F. Kennedy on pages 81–82 of the Student's Book. Talk about the text with a friend, trying to use the words or phrases above to explain what Kennedy is saying about the United States and its space programme.

Unit 5.3   Writing about evidence from an unseen source

When you decide whether evidence is weak or strong, you must remember to check a number of factors.

1 Here are the factors to consider when deciding on the strength or weakness of evidence. In each case, add an explanation of what each means, or of what you would want to check or ask. The first one has been done for you.

Factors

a the authors and their background

 Are they experts? Are their views reliable – might they be biased?

b the context/background of the text

c use of commentators or 'witnesses', or of other sources, in the text

d balance of evidence

e relevance or plausibility of evidence

f use of data and statistics

2 Read this short paragraph from a business magazine produced in India.

> It is undeniable that women are as capable as men around the world of developing and leading multi-million dollar businesses. In our own country, take the example of Kiran Mazumdar Shaw, generally recognised as India's wealthiest female entrepreneur, whose biopharmaceutical firm, Biocon, which she founded in 1978, has made her India's 54th richest person. The revenue of the company is an astonishing 48.85 billion rupees.

a What point or perspective is the article trying to promote or put forward?

b What evidence is provided to support this point?

c How strong or weak is it? Using the pages at the back of the Workbook or a separate piece of paper, make notes on whether the source uses each of the following, and what this suggests.

- expert or official sources
- relevant or reliable data/statistics
- balanced or unbalanced evidence
- relevant or plausible evidence.

3   **Now, complete this paragraph on the strength of the evidence, using the pages at the back of the Workbook or a separate piece of paper.**

The author of the article asserts that women are as successful in running big businesses as men globally. The author cites the example of…

and provides evidence of her success through…

The evidence here is weak / strong because…

Key terms and language support

You will have already learned that using direct quotations from a source text is an important way of indicating your understanding or explaining a point. However, remember the following:

When quoting a smaller section of text, 'embed' it in your own words, making sure it flows grammatically. For example: *A recent article in India At Work (1) claims that Kiran Mazumdar Shaw, is <u>'generally recognised as India's most wealthy female entrepreneur'.</u>*

Note the use of quotation marks for the exact words lifted from the original text and how these have been slotted into the sentence.

You could also selectively pick out related words or phrases from a source if you wished to emphasise a point. For example: *The article provides evidence of Shaw's success from her being India's <u>'54th richest person'</u> to the value of her business which is <u>'48.85 billion rupees'</u>.*

If you are quoting a longer section of text, you would normally introduce it, then leave a space before inserting the section required. However, in an assessment situation you are more likely to use the shorter form.

Task 4

Practise your use of direct quotation by looking at one of the sources you have identified. Make a simple point introducing the perspective in one of the ways shown above.

_____

_____

_____

_____

_____

_____

_____

_____

_____

_____

_____

_____

Reflection

Look at any of the texts or other pieces you are using as part of your own research and select a paragraph at random. Practise the process of identifying the point of view and then the different types of evidence used by the writer. Make your own assessment of how strong or weak it is.

Unit 5.4 Evaluating arguments and perspectives from two sources

Evaluating arguments and perspectives in two texts requires you to be clear and concise in the way you compose your writing.

Read these two extracts from articles about working women.

Document 1

Report from [...] University, Business department

Around the world, our research has shown that approximately 50% of working age women are part of the labour force, demonstrating their importance to global trade and local economies. And, in third level education (for example, university or college study), there are now more women than men in every region except Africa, and even here it is a very small margin. All this shows that women are more than capable of achievement across the board.

But there is a problem at the very top level. Nowhere in the world do women occupy more than 40% of managerial positions – and in many parts it is closer to 20%. Men dominate and continue to prevent women from gaining an equal foothold.

[source: ILOSTAT]

Document 2

Blog by successful woman entrepreneur

Imposter syndrome is the feeling people get that they do not deserve their success and that they might be 'found out' or revealed to be a fraud. For example, at least 65% of women running their own businesses said they suffered from 'imposter syndrome' according to a recent survey. I can vouch for that. Often, I have been overwhelmed by nerves when about to address a conference or lead a presentation, even on a topic in which I'm an expert.

It is interesting that men do not suffer from imposter syndrome in the same way as women. Where women seem to feel vulnerable and wounded, men automatically erect a shield of invincibility and are always well-armed for battle. Women, then, are their own worst enemies.

---

1 Answer these questions.

a What is the main/shared focus of both texts?

_____

_____

_____

b In what way do the two texts differ in their perspectives? How do you know?

_____

_____

_____

Look at the evidence in each case.

a   Use this table to make notes of the points made in each document. The first ones have been done for you. You will need to complete this using the pages at the back of the Workbook or a separate piece of paper.

Document 1	Document 2
Globally, labour force = 50% women/ 50% men – women important to trade, etc.	65% of women in survey suffer 'imposter syndrome'

b   You should also add a brief note about how weak/strong the argument is in each of these points. For example:

Document 1: No figures to back up assertion of women's contribution to 'the economy' – assumes women working more productive than if not.

 Using the pages at the back of the Workbook or a separate piece of paper, summarise how convincing you find the arguments in each case. Look at the 'Key terms and Language support' box first. Follow this plan:

Introduction: summary of the topic(s) and the two articles' focuses

Body of the text: compare the two texts, their perspectives and the arguments

Conclusion: say which is more convincing, in your view, and why

Note: This is a shortened and less detailed version of the sort of response you might make in an exam.

Key terms and language support

A useful structure when you are commenting on texts is to use phrases such as 'I think' or 'The source shows' plus 'that'.

For example, you could write:

The article reveals / shows / suggests that…

Task 4

After you have finished Task 3, underline any examples where you used this structure.

Reflection

Share your 'mini-essay' with a friend. Compare the points you made and how fluently you switched between the two documents.

Unit 6.1 Choosing a topic

It is important you choose a topic that engages YOU – one that you WANT to learn more about while also considering different points of view.

1 **Consider these questions and make notes in the graphic organiser below.**

   a What am I interested in?

   b Why am I interested? What motivates me?

   c What is the controversy? What perspectives/themes can I see?

Controversy

_____
_____
_____

Topic

_____
_____
_____

Perspectives

_____
_____
_____

Why?

_____
_____
_____

Motivation

_____
_____
_____

2 **How does my topic lead to a question?**

Copy the template, using the pages at the back of the Workbook or a separate piece of paper, and fill it in with your ideas.

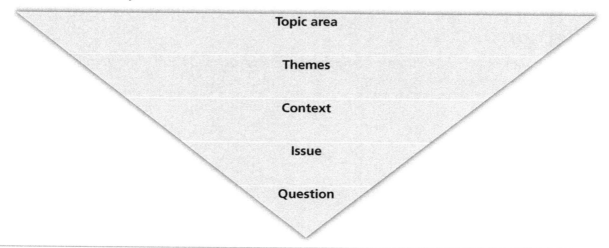

Topic area

Themes

Context

Issue

Question

3 **How far are your choices:**

- relevant – do they fit your interest and scope for research?
- global – have you included perspectives from around the world?
- debatable – do they create debate and different viewpoints?
- accessible – will you be able to explore your research further?

Tick the boxes that apply.

	Topic 1	Topic 2	Topic 3	Topic 4	Comments
Topic area/issue					
Relevant					
Global					
Debatable					
Accessible					

Key terms and language support

Task 4

In the Student's Book, this unit features a number of idioms related to choosing topics. Some of them are underlined in the examples below. Using the pages at the back of the Workbook or a separate piece of paper, explain what each of them means.

a It helps to <u>put yourself in the shoes of</u> someone with a different perspective.

b The subject was clearly <u>off limits</u> when I suggested it to my teacher.

c Some issues <u>stir up deep feelings</u> so need to be handled carefully.

d There are certain <u>pitfalls</u> you need to watch out for when selecting topics.

e What ideas can you <u>come up with</u>?

Reflection

The Reflective plenary in the Student's Book asks you to make a note of any initial obstacles or challenges you might meet in exploring your topic. Write down key actions you could take to resolve them and add a time/date by which you will do so.

Unit 6.2   Time management

Rome was not built in a day – and nor is your essay completed in a day. While you may have a number of weeks or months for the task, it is important to allocate sufficient time to all the parts of the essay.

1   **Unlike an 'exam' essay, you have plenty of time for this coursework essay, but it is still important to plan and use that time well.**

Make notes on how long you expect to work on each aspect of the essay. Some aspects may work concurrently, but you do need to finalise certain things at key points.

- Topic and question selection _____
- Research for background to topic _____
- Research for evidence for topic _____
- First draft _____
- Second draft _____
- Editing essay structure _____
- Adding references and bibliography _____
- Proofreading and checking _____

2   **Use this table to plan your essay.**

Section of essay	Task	Start	Planned end date	Deadline	Comment
Preparation	Topic selection				
	Question				
	Research				
	Planning				
Writing	First draft				
	Introduction				
	Perspective 1				
	Perspective 2				
	Perspective 3				
	Reflection				
	Conclusion				
	Second draft				

Finalising	Editing (for overall shape)				
	Proofreading				
	Editing (structure and word count)				
	Inserting references				
	Bibliography				
	Final proofreading				
	Final check of bibliography				
	Final check – word count/ layout				
	Submission				

Key terms and language support

This is an appropriate time to review your understanding of the content headings from the table here, such as 'Perspective' and 'Bibliography'. Do not ignore words such as 'Submission', which are important in the context of meeting deadlines.

Task 3

Write down your own quick definitions of each, then check them against the definitions given by your teacher or in the Student's Book.

_____
_____
_____
_____
_____
_____
_____
_____
_____
_____

Reflection

When you have completed your table, share it with a group and/or your teacher to evaluate how realistic it is.

Unit 6.3   Research for your coursework essay

Research is a key factor for your essay – and it involves much more than doing a quick Google search! It is important that you are able to find, take notes on and evaluate relevant information.

Tasks 1 and 2 use Martin Luther King Jr.'s 'I have a Dream' speech, which is easily accessed in libraries or online. Ideally, research and use your own source to hone your skills. What is important is that you write your answers down.

1   **Use RAVEN to evaluate the speech or your own source.**

   a   How reliable is the source/author? _____
   _fsgnsljgnwjl_____

   b   Is the information first-hand or second-hand? _____
   _____

   c   Does anyone benefit materially from the source? _____
   _____

   d   Is the source objective or subjective? _____
   _____

2   **Now, using King's speech or, ideally, your own source, identify the key things you will need for effective notes.**

   a   Source title: _____

   b   Author: _____

   c   Date: _____

   d   Topic: _____

   e   Themes: _____

   f   Perspectives: _____
   _____

   g   Key quotations: _____
   _____

3   Are you able to be empathetic towards this subject? In other words, can you understand why others may care or feel strongly about it? Use the following table to decide how sensitive you are about your topic.

Topic	My view	My reaction to other views	Am I able to be empathetic?	Am I willing to shift my viewpoint?

Key terms and language support

Task 4

When looking at sources, a number of related terms are often used. Here are some notes on one source a student has found.

Guardian article on sound pollution <u>challenges</u> my initial perspective (nearly all marine pollution is due to plastic).

Have found <u>multiple sources</u> to <u>corroborate</u> my perspective but need to <u>incorporate</u> references to sound pollution in essay.

Need to decide if these are <u>contrasting</u> perspectives or <u>alternative</u> ones on marine pollution.

What do the underlined words in the notes mean in each case? Use the pages at the back of the Workbook or a separate piece of paper to write your answers.

Reflection

Think about the topic you are considering. Are you able to show empathy towards the views of people expressed as part of it? How willing are you to shift your viewpoint if the evidence emerges to challenge what you think?

Unit 7.1   Organising your ideas

The work for the essay is not about reinventing the wheel. Instead, you need to show that you can 'stand on the shoulders of giants', using research information to support your own argument.

1 **Write down the first three words that come to mind when describing your:**

a   topic   _____   _____   _____

b   issue   _____   _____   _____

2 **Now, extend these ideas by completing the mind-map opposite based on your question. Fill in the 'twigs' on each branch according to the labels.**

Key terms and language support

Although there is no need to include an abstract in your essay, it can be useful to draft one as a way of clarifying your ideas. An abstract usually consists of a summary of your work and includes:

• the general context or background to your question/topic

• the question itself and what you aimed to find out

• the outcomes from the research and other work you did.

Now, try to write an abstract for your essay.

Reflection

Are you able to write an abstract at this point? If not, ask yourself why. Is it because you are lacking information, or because you haven't drawn conclusions yet? Or some other reason? What will you need to do to resolve this?

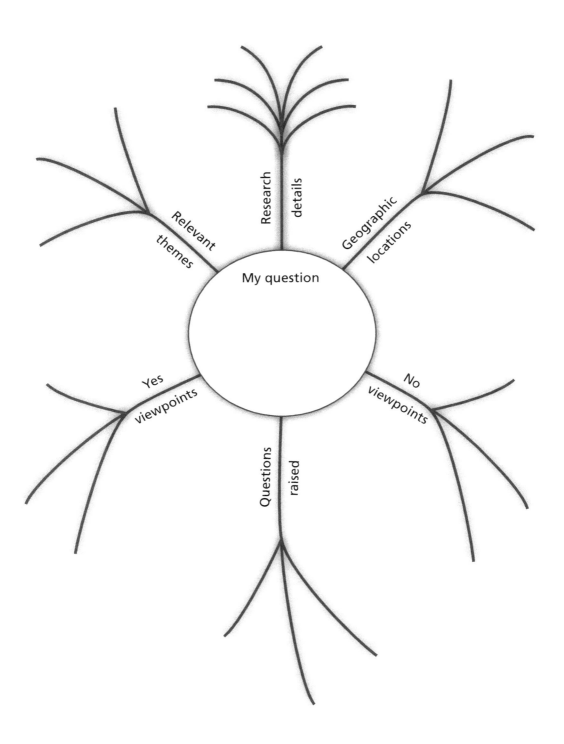

Unit 7.2 Structuring and preparing to write

Your essay needs to be planned carefully so that it has a clear shape that will lead the reader to the answer.

1 **Identify the function of each of the following extracts: explanation, description, reason, conclusion/perspective, contrast, motivation.**

   a Indigenous people are defined as those born in a specific location from parents similarly born.

   _____

   b The proposal for mining in a World Heritage site near me triggered my interest in the consequences of industrial development on the environment.

   _____

   c Because the site is in a rural area, it is important not to allow mining.

   _____

   d However, we live in a world where resources such as rare metals necessary in technology are increasingly hard to find.

   _____

   e The internet is a global tool of communication involving the use of the World Wide Web founded by Tim Berners-Lee.

   _____

   f Therefore, I believe that, yes, indigenous peoples should have a say in mining proposals.

   _____

2 **Be honest about your motivation for writing the essay. Can you write two versions (about 70 words each) to show why you chose your topic/question? Use the pages at the back of the Workbook or a separate piece of paper if you need more space.**

   a _____

   _____

   _____

   _____

   _____

   b _____

   _____

   _____

   _____

   _____

3 The structure of your essay needs to take into account the areas you were unable to address and where further research would be needed. Use the spider diagram below to note all the areas you could address, if space wasn't limited.

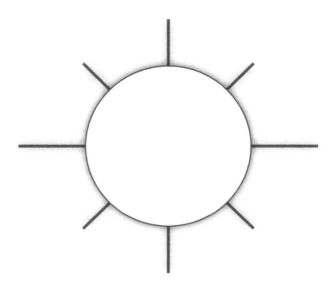

Now, sort your ideas into three tiers.

Top tier: the core areas your essay will address

_____

2nd tier: how each of these will be extended in more detail in the essay

_____

3rd tier: aspects you do not have space to cover but which you will mention and need further research

_____

Key terms and language support

The way you use tenses, adverbs and prepositions can help you to organise and structure your thinking. For example:

Initially, I thought that…   (adverb expressing past time + past tense verb)

However, I realised that…   (adverb expressing contrast/change + past tense verb)

Now, it seems that…   (adverb expressing present moment + present tense verb)

Task 4

How could you use this structure to explore different perspectives on your question or topic?

Reflection

Check over your own work to see how effectively you have used adverbs to structure your thinking. Could your work be improved by using a greater variety?

Unit 7.3   Writing, editing and referencing

A useful way to begin your essay is to 'back-write' – by starting with the conclusion.

1   **Allow yourself 15 minutes and start to write the conclusion to your essay, answering your question. Try to write 100–150 words. Use the pages at the back of the Workbook or a separate piece of paper if you need more space.**

_____

_____

_____

_____

_____

_____

_____

_____

_____

_____

_____

2   **Rewrite the following unsupported argument by inserting the evidence provided. (Note that the evidence is not in the correct order.) Use the pages at the back of the Workbook or a separate piece of paper if you need more space.**

> *The question I want to look at focuses on whether the dangers of plastic pollution outweigh those of chemical pollution. I was motivated by the problems at our beach. A quick scan showed that this was not an isolated problem. There is evidence that plastic pollution is easier to clean up than chemical pollution. Chemical pollution needs to be tackled at source and is much more expensive to deal with. Therefore, it is likely that chemical pollution poses more danger in the long term than plastic pollution.*

Evidence:

- plastic waste including bottles and masks
- the internet
- the local council
- factories or agricultural production processes
- a polluted river
- more labour
- LEDCs
- alternative uses for plastic rubbish.

_____
_____
_____
_____
_____
_____
_____
_____
_____
_____
_____
_____
_____
_____
_____
_____

Key terms and language support

It is useful to regularly practise your proofreading and referencing skills, so that good habits become the norm.

Task 3

Rewrite the following passage about school reports, correcting minor grammar and spelling errors, inserting any footnotes needed and creating a bibliography.

Reports, forming one strand of communication, can be considered critical to a schools image as they are sent to parents on a regular basis forming a most large part of "the public face of a school[]. Their is an controversial around school reports where parents seam to find them uninformed [] and schools consider them a important part of communication [].

Sources:

- _SEL Misiewicz, The Public Face of Reports, Harare, Roehampton Online, 2017_
- _AB Cade, Parents' Wishes and School Expectations, Brighton, Education Publishing, 2021_

_____
_____
_____
_____
_____
_____

Reflection

Look at the last piece of extended writing you did. What areas do you need to focus on with regard to spelling, punctuation, grammar or referencing? How could you improve these?

Unit 8.1   What is the Team Project?

Understanding the global relevance of problems, and the different roles that contribute to effective teamwork, will develop your communication and thinking skills.

 1 **Read this local problem and decide on the potential global relevance. Write notes and questions for further research, using the pages at the back of the Workbook or a separate piece of paper.**

> **Problem**
>
> We live in a very dry and almost desert-like area. Our river is drying out and disappearing. This is due to the fact that water is being diverted by the many local golf clubs to keep the grass green, as well as a jeans manufacturing company that uses the water in their manufacturing processes. Our reservoir is drying up, and animals and nature are suffering from this lack of water.
>
> **Global relevance?**
>
> e.g. The issue of access to water supplies affects people everywhere. Who is involved here?

2 **Read the descriptions a–l and decide which best fits team roles 1–12. Write the letter of the description next to the role below. The first one has been done for you.**

1 facilitator = a
2 strategy analyst
3 reflection coach
4 debater/devil's advocate
5 energiser or harmoniser
6 researcher

7 timekeeper
8 reporter
9 note-maker or recorder
10 language expert
11 leader, manager, chairperson
12 IT expert

a The person who helps everyone in a team work together better by making it easier to understand and achieve common goals and objectives.

b The person who makes sure that working time together as a team goes productively, who manages and shares tasks and deadlines, and solves problems.

c The person who establishes and checks facts and details, and who investigates evidence further.

d The person making notes to summarise meetings and accurately records work done, tasks and deadlines set by the group.

e The person who is able to think up objections to proposed arguments and counter-arguments in a constructive way, and has the ability to suggest alternative explanations and solutions.

f The person who manages and is aware of time limits and constraints, and who keeps the group on track with reminders.

g The person acting as the team's spokesperson, presenting summaries or conclusions of discussions to the class, other groups and the teacher(s).

h The person who has a good knowledge of how devices (i.e. mobiles, computers) and software programmes (i.e. presentation or video-editing tools) work and can teach others.

i The person who has a good command of written and spoken English and is able to help the team where needed.

j The person making sure the group stays positive, who expresses all ideas in a productive way, maintaining good working relationships.

k The person who makes sure that the team is on track by carefully analysing the successes and failures of different strategies and actions, and deciding how to operate next.

l The person who encourages the team to think about, analyse and consider individual and team strategies for achieving goals and deadlines.

Key terms and language support

Task 3

Read through Unit 8.1 again and identify any new and useful academic words, then work out all the word classes you can make from them. Remember that not all word classes will be possible for all words. Using the pages at the back of the Workbook or a separate piece of paper, create a visual or infographic to help you remember.

For example:

Noun
implication
relevance

Verb or language 'chunk'
to be implied in/by (someone/something)
to be relevant to (someone/something)

Adjective (and its opposite)
–
relevant/irrelevant

Adverb
implicitly
relevantly

Reflection

Which of the roles listed above do you usually take in group and team work?

Answer these questions to write an entry in your reflective log or journal.

- Which roles are you challenged by or want to avoid? Why?
- Which do you find easier/easiest? Why?
- Which role(s) are your best fit for the Team Project?
- Which combination of roles have you decided on for your Team Project? Why? How?
- Look at the diagram on page 128 of the Students' Book. What stage are you at in your team development? Give reasons and examples.

Unit 8.2 Selecting suitable problems to research

Identifying a local problem and systematically answering some key questions, exploring who and what is involved, will show you how globally relevant it is now – or might become in the future.

1 **Read the local problems below. Which are globally relevant and why (or why not)?**

  a The frog population (unique to one area near our college) is endangered, almost extinct. For example: *Globally relevant if the problem can be related to global animal extinction / loss of habitat.*

  b Some pupils in our school don't have the technology the teachers say they need.

  c Our regional roads are unsafe and traffic accidents kill thousands each year.

  d Wages are so low in our town that even people who have jobs are using food banks.

  e Some 'traditional healers' promise miracles so people consult and pay them, not doctors.

  f Women earn much less than men in all industries in our region.

  g Refugees and migrants are straining the resources of local government and charities.

2 **A student has made notes below (a–h) about problem 1a above, using the questions given in the framework below. Match the notes to the questions. Some of the notes relate to the same question and can relate to more than one question.**

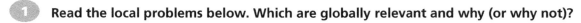

1. In what ways/how is it important (or not) **now**?	2. How was the issue important (or not) **in the past**?	3. How could it become important **in the future**?	4. **Who** are the stakeholders? Who benefits/gains? Who loses? How? In what ways?

Local problem or issue to solve

5. **Where** are these people affected? **When**? (now, in the future?)	6. In what way does it have **global impact or relevance**?	7. **What/whose perspectives** in addition to these could be used to examine the issues?	8. **What information** can be found through quick research in local languages and English?

  a This issue didn't exist in the past locally, as frogs were plentiful and reproduced in abundance every year. 2

  b Local stakeholders are the building and construction companies and their investors and shareholders who are all trying to build on the frog habitat to make a luxury hotel. Local stakeholders also include the residents who enjoy and love the frogs (important to our cultural and traditional spiritual beliefs). ☐

  c Global relevance is that over a third of amphibians are facing extinction worldwide. Impact? Medical losses – a round 10 per cent of Nobel Prizes for Medicine are based on frogs – their skin and gastric juices have substances that are/may be significant to pharmaceutical industries, e.g. antimicrobial and antibacterial properties that will become even more important as antibiotic resistance increases globally. ☐

d   Global stakeholders are the multinational hotel chain trying to build on the land and local government who say the project will provide local employment and develop international tourism. Affects local people, council, government and environment now, with further potentially negative effects in the future. ☐

e   Frogs are important food sources for their predators (monkeys, birds, fish) → biodiversity:
   • Tadpoles filter water drink to make it cleaner.
   • Frogs eat disease-carrying mosquitos (e.g. malaria, dengue fever) so reduce problems in local area. ☐

f   The global stakeholder groups will all benefit financially, but the hotel chain is based overseas and profits will not stay in the local area. The management of the hotel will be from their mother company in Spain, so knowledge will not be transferred, doesn't benefit locals, who lose out. ☐

g   Potential perspectives include these themes and topics: Sustainable futures, Urbanisation, Tourism (?), Animal rights (??), Health issues, Environmental priorities. ☐

h   These issues will carry on to the future, lower biodiversity, increased mosquito numbers and diseases they carry, less pure water, human/frog health is interlinked (as our traditional beliefs support). ☐

3   **Use the framework and the example notes above to develop your thinking about a local issue you have identified as globally relevant. Use the ideas in Task 1. Make notes, using the pages at the back of the Workbook or a separate piece of paper to answer the questions.**

Key terms and language support

Include some of these expressions in your team/individual statement to introduce and describe the local problem you have identified and explain its global relevance.

The local issue (we / I) selected is… / can be described as…	*The global relevance of this issue is (in no doubt / not to be underestimated / unmistakably)…*
It has been a source of (controversy / disappointment / conflict) for (some time / many years)	*(It / this issue) affects (countries / environments / populations / industries that / everyone who)…*
It is something our (community / city / country) is facing for the first time / must now consider due to…	*…has been the result of (recent debate / changes in the way)…*
The impact of our problem locally lies in (how / the way it affects…) the overall (health / access to)…	*A (further / future) potential (issue / impact / perspective) (is / might / could be)…*
	(We / I) will be exploring the (issue / problem) from a number of perspectives, including…

Reflection

Choose any of the issues in Task 1 or other local problems you have identified as likely to have global relevance. Select one or two for quick initial research. Practise the process of using different search engines to identify how long the local problem has existed for, how much has been published and if you can find related international material.

Unit 8.3 Preparing for your presentation

Evaluating information from different sources starts with a close examination of each publication you have identified. This involves key academic and life skills.

1 Read the extracts from student evaluations of different sources in Task 2 below. For each evaluation, note down which of the criteria listed are addressed and whether the evaluation has enough detail. You will need to use the pages at the back of the Workbook or a separate piece of paper.

    i fact/opinion

    ii objective/persuasive

    iii level of bias

    iv assumptions

    v up to date

    vi reliable

2 Now go through the evaluations again and underline any evidence or reasons why the sources may be useful.

    a Mainly contains facts, however some points are the author's opinion. It is objective because it considers both sides of the argument. It was published two years ago so it isn't the most recent. This is published by the sport federation, so it is probably reliable. For example: i, ii, v and vi are considered. More reasons/evidence for evaluation needed.

    b This is a report conducted by the Institute for Fiscal Studies; the information given is all facts and the report is persuasive. The opinion is neutral. Although the report was constructed before the event, it's still up to date. The prediction for the economic impacts on the EU are also very useful.

    c It is objective because it is based on fact with no level of bias or assumptions. It is not up to date as it was published in 2013, but is also reliable because the author is a professor.

    d This article's purpose is to provide knowledge, so it's written in an objective style and doesn't show any personal opinions. A lot of data is used that is collected from different sources. These must be checked. Assumptions are made based on the author's interpretation of historical events. The article is new, published this year, and the information doesn't date quickly. In conclusion I think this information source is reliable and useful. The website provides information to people involved in the industry and although it doesn't tell us everything, it provides general and objective knowledge to research further.

    e This document was based on facts that the writer conducted primary research for. It is well detailed and goes straight to the point.

    f This journal article is based on facts and analysis of the effect of depression in different parts of our society. It is objective, and explains the nature of the condition, including definitions symptoms and treatments. It uses data like statistics and cites a number of other sources in the form of quotations or paraphrases, which improves the level of reliability. It is not biased as it does not state any personal opinions.

3 Use this form to make notes evaluating the suitability of a source you are thinking of using in your presentation research. Copy the form separately if you need more space.

Name of website/book/article/journal	
Title of article/book	
URL	
Publisher of website/book	
Author of article	
Date of publication and last update	
Date accessed	
Type of website/book	
Evaluation of this source: • fact/opinion • objective/persuasive • level of bias • assumptions • up to date • reliable	

Key terms and language support

These expressions will help you present findings, opinions and evaluations of your sources:

As you can see from the data / tables / graphs in this article / source...
According to (this article / source)...
It can be seen from (this article / source) that...
Our / my first question / problem / issue / perspective / topic to research was... because...

Contrary to what we believed (initially), we / I discovered / found that...
Our findings suggest that / provide support for the argument / idea that...
In general / Overall it is possible that it is likely / unlikely that...
The local issue we identified raises interesting questions regarding...
However, the results of our initial research were not very encouraging and we conclude...

As the author points out (in this article / programme / video)...
According to Westcott / this article... / Westcott suggests that...

Reflection

Answer these questions to focus on metacognition:

• How successfully did I evaluate different sources of information? (How do I know?)

• What helped/stopped me from achieving the reading, research and evaluation tasks?

• What will I do differently in the next lesson(s)/the next time I need to read, research, evaluate information and sources?

Unit 8.4   Organising your argument

Use your notes and ideas from your research and reading to complete the content of your argument in order to generate your slides.

1 **Are you ready to organise your argument? Complete this checklist to identify any further action you need to take before moving on to the next stage.**

Task/objective	Deadline?	In progress? Complete?	Improvement needed?	Further action needed?
Identify, evaluate and select a variety of sources to research the local problem from a global perspective.				
Read and analyse texts (media and print-based) closely to identify any ideas of relevance.				
Make detailed notes to synthesise and summarise main points, possible arguments and evidence.				
Decide on and organise arguments. Select appropriate supporting evidence from research and investigate further if needed.				
Decide on possible solutions to the problem; discuss and compare the distinct perspectives.				

2 **Read the following extracts from some notes a student has made to organise their arguments. Which section of the presentation (a–e) on the next page does each note fit? Two of the notes fit the same section of the presentation.**

i   Show 10–20 seconds of video and tell the story of what the campaigners in a city in India achieved. For example: [e]

ii   Problem: overcrowded chaotic rush-hour traffic affecting productivity and quality of life. My sol. → banning the use of private cars in the city → environmental priority perspective of air and noise pollution because my cousin died (explain her story and the campaign we started in her honour). [ ]

iii   Outline the issue(s) and show mortality rates for our city/other cities comparable in size. [ ]

iv   Note that this relates to J's sustainable future, A's health issues and F's exploration of scientific innovation. [ ]

v   Use the historical records/data graphs of traffic volume, air pollution data to introduce my first argument (we must recognise and act individually). Quote Law and legal limits, and cite failures by local government (newspaper and meeting reports). [ ]

vi   Describe the fact our city is breaking the law, how this has come to be and why. [ ]

a Introducing local problem/the rationale for my perspective.
(What is the problem / global relevance? Why did you choose this way of looking at it? How does it link to the other team member's perspectives? How is it 'distinctive' and unique to you?)

b First section.
(What is the 'big picture'? What light does your perspective shine on the problem?)

c Analysing and evaluating the main point(s).
(Identify 5–6 main points from your research notes. What is the main message of each?)

d Communicating arguments, clarifying with supporting evidence.
(What are your arguments in relation to the solution you are proposing? How does each one relate to your main points and contribute to the solution? What evidence have you selected? How and what does it help the audience to understand?)

e Giving examples.
(Which examples can you identify to help make your arguments and evidence clear? How do these examples support your solution?)

3 **Make notes in answer to the questions in each section above to help organise your own argument. Use the pages at the back of the Workbook or a separate piece of paper.**

Key terms and language support

Task 4

Complete these sentences to expand your notes into arguments, using the pages at the back of the Workbook or a separate piece of paper.

The global relevance (of …) is…
Considering the problem from… perspective…
There are… main factors/issues/reasons that explain…
(One of) The main arguments (for/against) this idea/plan are…

As the author points out (in this article/programme/video of her presentation at the conference)…
According to Westcott/this article…
Westcott suggests that…
Although Westcott claims that…

Another way of looking at this issue is…
This is important because/due to the fact that…
In support of this theory/idea/solution is…
Here is a (graph/picture, etc.) that shows the way in which…
An (another/a further) example shows/demonstrates/is applicable to…

Reflection

Complete the tasks below to help you write a journal entry for your reflective log.

• What questions do you have about the arguments you are organising for your presentation? Write them down and try to research the answers. Ask your classmates and teacher.

• Visualise a member of your audience (i.e. teachers/classmates/examiners). Remember, they are not 'specialists'. Make a list of tricky questions that any of them might ask about the content of your presentation. Can you answer them?

• What has this task helped you to understand more about?

Unit 8.5   Using language to present effectively

Using language expressions that signpost or signal your intentions during a presentation will help your audience to follow your 'road map' easily, and to understand where you are going.

 1 The table below contains signpost expressions from a presentation about environmental pollution. Match the beginnings (a–j) with the grammatical and logically possible endings (i–x). There is more than one answer in some cases.

For example: *a iii*

Sentence starters that signpost or signal different sections or arguments in a presentation	Possible ways of ending one or more of the sentences
a I'd like to explain/expand on/discuss/demonstrate/elaborate on/look at…	**i** to put it bluntly, we are doomed if we fail to act now. Our future health relies on the availability of fresh, clean air.
b So, I'll conclude by…	**ii** close to 25 000 people's lives a year are negatively impacted by the harmful practices discussed in this section.
c I have explained why…	**iii** the issue of air pollution in relation to brain development in children and babies.
d In other words…	**iv** if we reduced our reliance on our cars we could save over 10 000 lives over a ten year period.
e Looking at this in more detail, we can see that…	**v** making my proposed solution acceptable to the older generation.
f So, according to these graphs included in the company's report…	**vi** inviting everyone to consider which of the examples given could work globally, and why.
g To illustrate the possible benefits of this approach…	**vii** that the existing alternatives are cheaper, more efficient and faster.
h The second reason is…	**viii** this argument has no merit, and is environmentally unsound.
i I'd like to focus on how to solve the problem of…	**ix** as Holstein suggests in her latest article, the prospect of doing nothing is morally indefensible.
j Taking an alternative view…	**x** the case has not been made clearly, and the suggested proposal uses incomplete and outdated statistics.

2   Into which sections of a presentation could the signpost expressions a–j in Task 1 fit? There are up to six possible answers in some cases. Write the numbers next to the correct headings in the table below.

Outline of sections	Outline of sections
Greeting/welcome Introducing topic and rationale e.g. *a*	Giving examples
	Completing a section
Outline of presentation structure	Introducing the different sections of your presentation
Introducing a section	
Analysing and evaluating the main point(s)	Summarising
Communicating arguments, clarifying with supporting evidence	Closing Coming to conclusions

Key terms and language support

Task 3

Look at these further signpost sentence starters and match a–d under the correct heading of the presentation structure in Task 2.

a
> To follow on/Next, I'll…
> Then…
> After that…
> Next…

b
> To sum up, then…
> To summarise (what I am proposing/ suggesting/saying here)…

c
> To begin with…
> First of all, I'd like to start by…

d
> My presentation is divided into four sections. I'll begin by… move on to… then I'll… and finally I'll…

Now write your presentation script, using the pages at the back of the Workbook or a separate piece of paper. Practise the process of linking the content and stages together under the different headings using these signposting expressions and useful ways to start and end sentences. Use the success criteria below.

Reflection

Look at the first draft of your presentation script. Make your own assessment of how well you have achieved the success criteria by highlighting the parts of your draft that answer these questions.

Where in your presentation script do you:

- provide a solution for the problem you researched?
- give a distinct perspective?
- use signpost language and a logical structure?
- make arguments and points clearly with evidence/examples?

Read your script aloud. Does it take more/less than 10 minutes?

Unit 8.6   Supporting your presentation visually

Your presentation slides need to communicate effectively through text and visuals.

1 Look at the grammar and punctuation tips in the Key terms and language support section to correct these draft versions of presentation slides.

A

Possible solutions include:

- The manufacture of local desalination plants which
  - o provide employment
  - o reduce reliance on international aid
1 The use of reverse osmosis and wind power.
2 Recycling human waste.
3 Collection of rainwater.

B

HUMAN GENETIC MODIFICATION

Arguments against proposed law

- creating perfect 'designer' babies → culling the weak?
- Gender – population not balanced!
- unforeseeable consequences…
- Lack of existing regulation.
- Religious groups are in opposition.
- views of future babies not modified 'enslaved' workers or inferior race?

2 Would these slides benefit from visual support? If so, what and why? Write your ideas down, using the pages at the back of the Workbook or a separate piece of paper.

For example: in A, key words could be in bold or underlined.

3 Use your script to draft these sections of your presentation. Add any notes about suitable visuals. Use your own digital slides, the pages at the back of the Workbook or a separate piece of paper if you need more space.

Introduction (topic, rationale, perspective)

Solution (with examples)

Summary of key points

Argument 1 (with supporting evidence)

Key terms and language support

Use these tips for making bullet points to help you draft your slides.

1   Choose which bullet points you need to make – lists, steps, stages, reasons, etc.

2   Use the same font for each slide, and emphasise with italics, bold or underline sparingly.

3   Use a spellchecker.

4   The text in each bullet point should start with a capital letter and end with a full stop (.), question mark (?) or exclamation mark (!) only if it is a complete sentence.

5   Keep the number of words to a minimum. You are going to explain and make the points orally in a more elaborate way. These key words keep your audience's attention.

6   Try not to use more than five bullet points on one slide. Will an image work better? Sometimes having images to talk about is more engaging for the audience to look at as they listen.

7   Be consistent in the grammar structures you use, i.e. don't mix a list with questions, sentences or parts of a sentence. Keep the same form in each.

8   Starting with the same part of speech can have more visual impact, e.g. verbs in active tenses for solutions or actions. For example:
    My proposed action plan to stop bullying on social media at our school includes:
    • educating parents/guardians
    • teaching and modelling responsible use
    • creating a school policy
    • inviting the community to help.

Reflection

Once you have planned/drafted your slides, produce them properly. Now, evaluate how successful they are.

• Are the bullet points and text/visuals clear and easy to read? (large enough? the same font? any use of italics, bold, underlining to emphasise key words? bullet points grammatical and logical?)

• Is the layout of the slide design balanced? (colour, amount of text/image types?)

• How/What does the visual information add to your message?

Use your answers to help you write an entry in your reflective log or journal.

Unit 8.7 Practice and evaluation

'Practice makes perfect', as the saying goes. You will gain confidence when you are sure of your material, your slide and script content and, above all, the message you want to give.

1 Read the advice below to help you with your presentation. Decide if a–f are true (T), false (F) or if there is no information in the text (?).

> **Presentation preparation**
>
> Whether you are recording a presentation or giving it in front of a live audience, you may feel equally nervous. What can you do to help yourself feel calm and confident? The best advice is simple: relax, you've got this! Yes, really! If you have read Student's Book, Chapter 8, followed all the advice, participated in and completed the tasks (including those in this Workbook), ticked all the boxes in your checklists and prepared your slide deck, you are good to go!
>
> Now your content is clear, your slides and script are ready, success lies in the way that you prepare yourself, both mentally and physically, in the days and night before you give your presentation. In the run-up to the big day, the tried and tested regime of effective public speakers include all the following: a good night's sleep, fresh air, exercise, healthy food including lots of vegetables, fruit, fish and, most importantly, hydration for your brain, body and your throat (use warm not cold water).

a The text is aimed at an audience of professional public speakers. For example: [F]

b The writer suggests that readers are not ready to present. [ ]

c The writer's tone is positive and encouraging to presenters. [ ]

d Readers are encouraged to start a diet. [ ]

e Eating fish is good for your brain. [ ]

f Drinking lots of water is something presenters should do. [ ]

2 Fill the gaps using the words from the box below to complete the presentation success criteria.

> understand present communicate researched volume non-specialist different

a Could the audience _understand_ and hear you clearly (i.e. sufficient _____)?

b Did you give a solution for the problem you _____?

c Did you _____ your arguments clearly in each section (logical structure)?

d Was your perspective clearly _____ from those of other team members?

e Did you explain ideas so that a _____ audience understood?

f How long did you _____ for (i.e. was it more than 7 minutes but less than 10)?

Key terms and language support

You could use any of the following phrases to open and close your presentation and engage your audience. Read them aloud and try out different ways of saying the words.

Who here today, believes / feels...?
Hands up if you believe / think / feel...
[Play an audio sound effect related to your presentation] Did you hear that sound? Well that was / will be...

So, before I close, let's review the reasons / arguments / solution...
The clock tells me it's time to close, so I'll...
Let me finish by saying...

Reflection

Make and use a recording of your presentation to evaluate. Make your own assessment of how well you have achieved the success criteria by answering the questions in Task 2.

Use your answers to help you write an entry in your reflective log or journal.

Unit 9.1 Reflection and reflective models

It is important to understand how reflective models can help structure your thinking.

1 **There are a number of pieces of advice in the Student's Book that you might find useful when thinking about reflection. In each case below, write down what you understand the underlined words or phrases to mean.**

   a Reflection is an <u>iterative process</u>.

_____

_____

   b It's important to have a <u>reflective mind-set</u>.

_____

_____

   c You should follow a <u>reflective cycle</u>.

_____

_____

   d <u>Self-questioning</u> is an integral part of the reflective process.

_____

_____

   e Reflective models tend to include an <u>action plan</u>.

_____

_____

2 **Gibbs' reflective cycle, shown here, is made up of a number of related and interconnected aspects.**

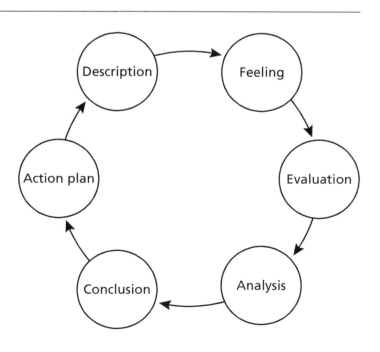

Match these sample reflective questions to each stage of Gibbs' model. Write each letter against the relevant part of the diagram.

a   What happened? What did I do? Who was there?

b   How did I feel during the situation or moment? How do I feel now? How do/did others feel?

c   Being objective, what went well? What wasn't successful? What was good? What was bad?

d   Why did that go well? Why did that go badly? Why did I perform in that way? What additional knowledge is or was needed to understand the situation?

e   What have I learned overall? What inferences can I draw from the process as a whole about what worked and didn't work? What would make the experience more positive? Are there other things I could have done?

f   What do I need to do now? What steps or strategies do I need to put in place the next time? What is my plan?

3 **Although the focus here is on your own Team Project, how might a model like Gibbs' reflective cycle be used in a national or global crisis or situation (such as the COVID outbreak)? Write a paragraph saying how it might be useful.**

_____

_____

_____

_____

_____

Key terms and language support

When you reflect, you are measuring your own understanding (or lack of it). What sort of language is useful in order to clarify the extent of your development?

Look at this example:

I have <u>significantly</u> improved my understanding of the market forces that underpin island communities.

Similar adverbs: *sufficiently / insufficiently; slightly / mostly; comprehensively / inadequately; entirely; wholly; (also not entirely / not completely to show understanding is not perfect).*

Task 4

Write a similar sentence (or sentences) in which you use these adverbs, which help with auditing your understanding on your own topic. Or evaluate your writing at a later stage to see whether such a formulation could help your explanations or analysis.

_____

_____

Reflection

What do you think the most challenging aspects of the process of reflection are? Why?

Unit 9.2 Reflecting on collaboration

Reflecting on the different elements of collaboration is key to a successful reflective paper.

 Here are a number of statements made by one student as part of their reflection on the collaborative process. Match each one to the different elements of the Gibbs model.

Elements: *description, feeling, evaluation, analysis, conclusion, action plan*

Student example	Element
I was unsure, initially, about sharing my personal experiences of trolling on social media, but it emerged that all of us had suffered similar experiences to a greater or lesser extent. This reassured me and I felt able to articulate some of my concerns.	
Problems began to emerge in the first meeting around our choice of topic. It was too large in scope and we struggled to stick to a core idea. We were all committed to the topic, but this also meant we pitched in with lots of ideas and information that we found difficult to refine into one more focused issue.	
Our group (Adil, Jamie, Jo and me) collaborated on exploring the effects of social media on teenagers' well-being. We scheduled meetings for every Wednesday after our class.	
Overall, the core things I learned were that sharing your own experiences can enhance trust within a group, but there also needs to be a time when the group steps back and looks at the process objectively, asking – what do we need to find out? What is our core focus? What is our timetable?	
In the future, I will approach collaborative work in a more measured way, helping my team assign roles from the start, setting goals and dates using appropriate channels of communication, and most importantly, setting out as a group core expectations and good practice (such as refining ideas before they lead us off on tangents).	
If we had begun by coming to the meeting with a suggestion of a more limited field to explore, we would not have been diverted into huge and often irrelevant discussions. In a sense, our enthusiasm and personal feelings didn't allow us to take an objective approach. Once we established a local focus – correlations between self-harm and cyber-bullying in the Bay City area, we were much more focused.	

2   **When writing about collaboration, how would you rank these different pointers in terms of importance? Choose 1 for the most important, 5 for the least important.**

a   being honest about your experience ☐

b   being able to pinpoint specific effective and less effective elements of the collaboration ☐

c   understanding why something worked or didn't work ☐

d   having an overall understanding of the whole process ☐

e   learning from the experience for future collaboration or teamwork ☐

Key terms and language support

You can use tenses to help you explain clearly and demonstrate your self-reflection. For example, note the use of three main tenses here:

I <u>had believed</u> [1] that power stations <u>were</u> [2] not particularly susceptible to water damage, but I comprehensively <u>altered</u> my outlook [2] after reading research into the meltdown of the core reactors at Fukushima in 2011. Now, <u>I recognise</u> [3] that flood surges are a major concern for communities.

[1] past perfect tense: an action completed in the past – often with some distance before another past event happened: *had* + past participle

[2] past simple tense: action completed before now: subject + past participle

[3] present tense: action or feeling now: subject + present form of verb

Task 3

Taking any prior thoughts or beliefs about a topic you have researched, construct a paragraph using the same format: past perfect tense – past simple – present simple.

You may need to add time markers or signposts ('At the start of my research…', etc.).

_____

_____

_____

_____

_____

_____

_____

_____

_____

Reflection

Which of the elements in Task 2 do you find the most difficult to write about? Why do you think that is?

Unit 9.3 Writing the Reflective Paper

The Reflective Paper must show sustained and structured evaluation of the collaborative process and of the learning journey.

 Read the following extract in which a student explains part of their 'learning journey'.

> I had become interested in issues related to social media and well-being after a friend of mine began to miss school due to online abuse. Even though I thought I understood the issue, it was only after I'd researched a wider range of causes that drive teenagers to use social media to fill perceived voids in their life that I realised it was a more complex issue. I had thought it was nothing to do with us but was purely a personal matter of will-power, but now I see that local factors – such as lack of investment in youth services or the decline of team sports – also contribute to the impact of social media for good or bad.

a Underline the sentence or sentences where the student identifies their prior understanding before they researched further.

b Highlight where the student explains what they did to gain better understanding.

c Circle the sentence or section where the student explains what they learned from their changed approach.

 In the paragraph above, the student uses a logical point and language structure:

What they thought originally and how they became interested	What changed after they widened their research	What they learned as a result
('I had become…' to show initial thoughts)	('it was only after…' to show progression in their thinking)	('now I see…' to show current understanding)

These sentences by a student working on a related topic are rather muddled. Sort them out so they follow a logical structure similar to the one above, using signposting words or phrases. You may need to add and take out words. Use the pages at the back of the Workbook or a separate piece of paper.

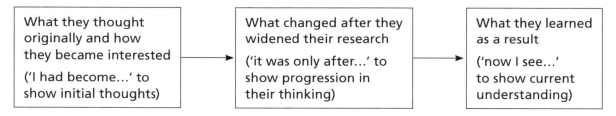

> By looking online, I was able to identify a number of reports into cyber-bullying globally. They were useful but I needed something local.

> Using new search terms, I found some local news articles in the 'Island Times' about social media and well-being. I made notes from these.

> I cross-referenced to the issues I'd heard friends and others talking about. I did my own survey.

Chatting to friends and other students about cyber-bullying was where I began my research – that wasn't enough.

By mixing data drawn from online reports and local surveys I gained a better picture of the problem.

Key terms and language support

When you write up reflections, you need to make sure your writing is clear but not stilted or lacking fluency. One aspect worth considering is participle endings.

Example A: I was organising the group's meetings, and setting the agenda for what we were discussing. It was important to be evaluating the sources we were choosing.

Example B: I organised the group's meetings and set the agenda for what we discussed. It was important to evaluate the sources we chose.

Task 3

a What differences do you notice in the verb forms in each example?

_____

_____

b Which of these two extracts is clear and has impact? Which one sounds rather repetitive and less precise?

_____

_____

Task 4

Look at examples of your own work and anywhere you use verbs ending in '-ing'. Where you can, try replacing them with the simpler form – does it improve your writing and make it clearer?

Reflection

Practise writing logical paragraphs, reflecting on any aspect of your work in the Team Project. Try a structure where you start with what you knew at first, what made you change or reconsider, and finish with what the outcome was and what you learned. Practise using a range of signposts related to time and consequence ('Before', 'Later', 'As a result', etc.).

Chapter 10 The Cambridge Research Report

Unit 10.1   Understanding the task

It is important that you understand the core requirements of the Cambridge Research Report.

1   **Here are some statements about the requirements of the Cambridge Research Report.**

Tick all those that are correct. Two are incorrect.
The report must:

a   be based on a single question that is appropriate for in-depth research

b   be written for a specialist audience – for example, if on a science topic, it should be aimed at scientific experts or professionals

c   be no more than 5000 words

d   be accompanied by a research log, tracking the work you did

e   demonstrate AO1 and AO2 skills, but not AO3

f   include a bibliography and full bibliographical references.

2   **Correct the two statements from Task 1 that are incorrect.**

_____

_____

_____

_____

3   **In the Student's Book, it states that the report will address both subject-appropriate and generic elements.**

Here are some aspects that one student is considering as part of their work on the report.

Circle those that could be considered 'generic' and underline those that are more 'subject-specific'.

Structuring the report effectively	Reflecting on research findings
Using a research log	Comparing contrasting perspectives
Assessing sources	Writing fluently in continuous prose
Using methodologies appropriate to that field	

Key terms and language support

The noun 'methodology' is an academic term used to mean the over-arching approach used in research or information-gathering. 'Methods' refers to the specific actions taken as part of the overall approach – for example, surveys or interviews. The words are almost interchangeable, but 'methodology' connotes the overall strategy and process undertaken. English is full of related words like this, which subtle nuances of meaning are important.

Task 4

How do the following terms differ, if at all? Is it simply a matter of everyday versus academic language? Are there clues in the spelling?

a 'technological' and 'technical'

_____

_____

b 'physiological' and 'physical'

_____

_____

c 'ideological' and 'idealistic'

_____

_____

Reflection

Check over the list of skills for the Cambridge Research Report as set out on page 24 of the syllabus. Evaluate your own level of mastery of each of them on a scale of 1 (low) to 10 (high). Discuss with your supervisor or teacher how you can address the specific weaknesses, if any, that you have identified.

Unit 10.2   Writing the proposal

Your proposal is an essential guide to how you will approach the Cambridge Research Report, so it is worth spending time on and ensuring it covers the core elements you will explore.

The Student's Book sets out some of the key aspects you might address in the proposal you submit to your supervisor or teacher. Here is one of them, related to the way in which you might carry out research, expressed as a spider diagram.

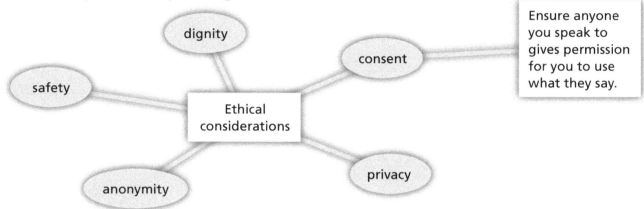

1. **What might these mean in practice? Copy the diagram, using the pages at the back of the Workbook or a separate piece of paper, and add your own explanations or linking words to the diagram, similar to the one shown for 'consent'.**

2. **Create your own spider diagram to explore the scope of your proposal, using the format above.**

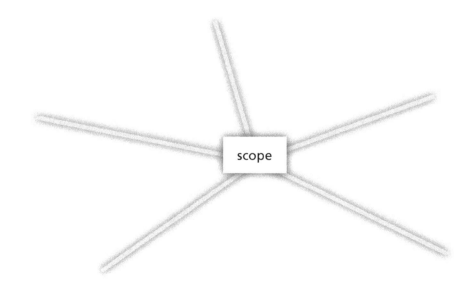

Key terms and language support

Any sort of proposal is likely to include language that tells the reader what you plan to do or defines key terms. For example:

> *In this essay, I will be using De Bono's 'Thinking Hats' [1] theory to explore how education has adopted these approaches in the classroom.*

Or

> *At various points in this essay I use the term 'Thinking Hats' to refer to De Bono's classic theory of the brain. [1]*

Other structures might include:

> *I want to (ask / explore) (how / why / whether)…*
>
> *I (wish / plan / intend) to…*
>
> *I will (examine / analyse)…*
>
> *I will seek to…*
>
> *I (ask / explore)…* etc.

Sometimes, you might use a relative clause beginning with 'which', 'whose' or 'that' to extend the definition or explanation:

> *I will be using De Bono's 'Thinking Hats' [1] theory, which suggests the brain thinks in six distinct ways, to explore how education has adopted these approaches in the classroom.*

Task 3

Write a sentence or two from an introduction or proposal for your Cambridge Research Report or any essay you are working on, which requires you to define a key term or idea. Try to use the structures above, and include a relative clause to add more detail.

_____

_____

_____

_____

_____

Reflection

What concerns you most about your proposed topic? Set out your concerns and think about how you could tackle them – is it a question of not being able to access information? Concerns about your own organisational skills? In each case, note down the challenge and a potential solution – or where you might go for support or help.

Unit 10.3 Research log

Your research log should be a working document that assists you in writing a better report. Recognising what it should and shouldn't include is vital.

1 **Which of the following things should you include in your research report? Tick those that should be included; put a cross against those that shouldn't.**

Feature	Yes/no
Full details of sources included	
A record of the number of hours you spend online	
How the perspectives or sources compare	
The times of day you log on to your computer	
Key concepts and arguments in the area of your research	
Questions you identify for further research	
How many times you visit the library	
A review of your research methods and methodology	
The number of classes that you attend	

2 **Read this extract from one student's log, then answer the questions on the next page.**

Draft title	Has 'trickle-down' economic practice helped the poorest in society?	
Date and source	**Comments**	**Next action**
16/12/2020 Businessinsider.com Article by Grace Dean	Secondary source, quoting a study by London School of Economics and King's College, London. Article refers to two views – tax-cuts for the wealthy that encourage investment, which then 'trickles down' in various ways to benefit others. The counter view – from the report – shows that this creates income inequality and has no effect on economic growth. I read and made brief notes on the source and its key findings.	Research the background to 'trickle-down' economics? Who coined the phrase? Lots of other reports mentioned in the article – do I need to read those, too? The article mentions many countries' tax policies – is my scope too wide? Do I need to refine my question?

a How many aspects from the list in Task 1 are included here? Note down each one, using the pages at the back of the Workbook or a separate piece of paper, and cross-reference it to the log. For example:

Full details of source included?
Date – 16/12/2020
Source: businessinsider.com
Author: Grace Dean

Note that the title of the article is missing, however.

b What evidence is there in the log that the question the student has selected is not necessarily their final one?

_____

c Why do they think they might need to change it?

_____

3   **What other information about the source has the student not commented on?**

_____

_____

_____

Key terms and language support

You have already had some guidance on note-making and there is more on this in 10.5, but remember that you can note things concisely and clearly by adopting a few basic techniques:

- Where meaning remains clear, leave out articles, determiners, prepositions, for example:

  'Article refers to two views' rather than '*The* article refers to two views'.

- Use abbreviations such as 'LSE' rather than 'London School of Economics', if the context is clear.

- Use bullets, highlighting and colours to separate out or emphasise information.

Task 4

Improve these notes made by one student, using the techniques above.

I listened to an interview on the British Broadcasting Corporation on 8 December 2020 in which Sir Richard Richman claimed that his business empire benefited the whole community. He also claimed that using tax avoidance measures was not illegal.

Start:

Interview on... _____

_____

_____

Reflection

In the Student's Book you were asked to start drafting your own log. By this point, you may have already begun it. If so, take a critical look at it and see if it needs refining at all – are there additional headings, columns or a different layout that you should consider?

Unit 10.4   Identifying a topic

Choosing an appropriate topic and question for your Cambridge Research Report is vital in making sure you give yourself the best chance to demonstrate the required skills.

1 **A suitable topic should be one that... (tick all that apply)**

   a allows you to explore concepts ☐

   b is very specific and obscure ☐

   c already has a substantial body of research you can investigate ☐

   d is linked to your interests and/or studies ☐

   e enables you to take an academic approach ☐

   f is very general ☐

   g you are incredibly passionate about ☐

   h allows synthesis of arguments ☐

   i is achievable (you can actually complete it) ☐

   j builds two contrasting perspectives. ☐

2 **'Concepts' are a core element of the report. These can be defined relatively simply as 'abstract ideas' – for example, the concept of the 'divine right of kings' in relation to the authority of sovereigns is the idea that monarchs are answerable to god or gods (having been chosen by them) before parliament or government – an issue at the heart of the French Revolution. This would be a concept worth exploring through research within the topic 'political power and resistance'.**

Here are three further topics. Choose one of them and suggest at least one concept you could, or would need to, explore.

- Medical ethics and priorities

- Crime

- Transport.

_____

_____

_____

3 **A student studying A Level Psychology, and who wants to do charity work, has devised the following question for their report.**

Is the main purpose of the criminal justice system to reform or punish offenders?

On the basis of the attributes for a good topic and question you identified in Task 1, is this a suitable choice?

Yes, it is a suitable choice because

_____

_____

Or

No, it is not a suitable choice because

_____

_____

Key terms and language support

Learning how to ask yourself questions is a key part of the course, but how you frame those questions can help you to choose fruitful topics.

Here are some possible question stems and how they might be used.

Did I / Have I…? Useful for looking back at what has been done (or not).

Should I / we…? Tentative thoughts about taking a new approach or considering other paths.

Where / when…? Useful for being precise about whether a specific idea, piece of information or action is or has been taken ('When will I need to decide my final question?').

What else…? Useful for querying anything that has been omitted or that still needs to be done.

What if…? Useful for hypothesising.

Why…? Useful for reiterating your thought processes or decisions, or questioning a specific decision ('Why does this help me move my research forward?').

Am I…? Can be used in lots of ways but could also be useful for reflection ('Am I too close to this topic? Am I approaching the material in a biased way?').

Task 4

Consider the topic or material you are currently looking at. Try to write full questions using each of these question prompts – and then try to answer them. Did they help you refine or develop your thinking?

_____

_____

_____

_____

_____

_____

_____

_____

_____

_____

_____

Reflection

Jot down further concepts related to – or which inform – your chosen topic. How well do you understand them? Can you explain the concept simply and succinctly?

Unit 10.5   Primary research and the research process

You have already tackled research and the process you use to conduct it, but it is useful to review and revise your knowledge.

1 **Write your own definitions of the following terms.**

  a quantitative research

  _____

  _____

  b qualitative research

  _____

  _____

  c primary research

  _____

  _____

  d secondary research

  _____

  _____

2 **What do the acronyms RAVEN and CRAAP stand for?**

  RAVEN _____

  CRAAP _____

3 **Write a list of key points of advice that would help you and other students when making notes from research.**

  For each one, create an easy-to-remember logo, emoji or abbreviation to help you remember it.

  1 *Highlight carefully only what is relevant to your research.*

  _____

  _____

  _____

  _____

  _____

  _____

  _____

  _____

  _____

  _____

  _____

  _____

Key terms and language support

Distinguishing between some of the terms in this unit is not straightforward, but identifying the different forms of research or evidence in a text is a useful way of weighing up its strengths.

Task 4

In the following text, what different types of evidence/research can you identify?

In an interview which I conducted in May 2020, Ms Anita Khan, Principal of Dale College, told me that remote learning had proved 'extremely effective, with all students being able to access our online provision and live tutor-led sessions'. However, exam results in the following term dropped by 15% using norm-referencing and national measures for Cambridge IGCSE™ performance in Maths, English and Science (Inter-government Report, June 2021, Department of Education). Student-led chatrooms also provided evidence of disquiet amongst the student community with a number of posts stating that technical issues had limited their learning time, even though the general quality of the tutor sessions was considered good.

_____

_____

_____

_____

_____

_____

_____

_____

_____

_____

_____

_____

Reflection

Check your current research plans. What types of research are you currently doing, or planning to do? What is the balance between primary and secondary?

Unit 11.1   Planning for the Cambridge Research Report

There is no single way to plan for or structure your Cambridge Research Report, but it is vital to have a systematic idea of what you intend to do.

 There are a number of ways of organising or connecting ideas as part of the process of drafting your report. Here are three of them. Next to each one, jot down what you think is good about them – and what might be considered less useful.

   a Spider diagram: a diagram that shows a summary of facts or ideas, with the main subject or idea in a central circle and key facts or ideas on lines drawn out from it.

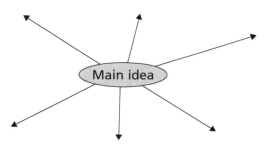

GOOD for...

NOT SO GOOD for...

   b Mind-map or word shower: a graphical display of ideas or topics linked in a non-linear way.

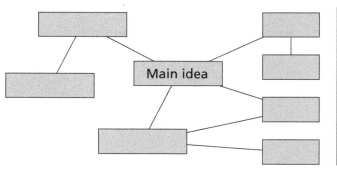

GOOD for...

NOT SO GOOD for...

   c Flow chart: a chart showing a process or sequence.

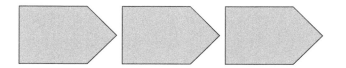

GOOD for...

NOT SO GOOD for...

The Student's Book also suggests using a diamond-shaped plan for a more linear structuring of your report.

What is the reason for using the 'diamond'-style plan? Note down how it helps you:

- separate out elements of the report
- give the right amount of time/space to different elements.

_____

_____

_____

_____

Key terms and language support

When generating ideas and structuring your report, it can be useful to apply a range of ways of thinking. Several terms (not ones you will necessarily ever need to write) may be useful in helping you articulate these approaches.

'The big picture' – this phrase is commonly used to help consider the whole goal and all the objectives you are trying to achieve. When you get slowed down by the detail, you can sometimes lose sight of this.

Task 3

What is the 'big picture' in terms of the work you are doing?

'Goals' versus 'objectives' – 'goals' usually define general guidelines for what you want to achieve, whereas 'objectives' tend to be measurable and defined by deadlines and dates.

Task 4

What are your goals? Are they the same as the 'big picture' or do you have personal goals which are separate to this?

What are your current objectives? If you don't have any, then it suggests your thinking may be a bit woolly or vague.

Moving between these 'macro' ways of thinking and planning to more 'micro' details is essential for success in creating your report.

Reflection

What type of learner are you? This question may help you think about how you plan and write. If you are someone who finds visualisation important then you might find the planning ideas in this section helpful. Or you might prefer to work orally/aurally, speaking aloud the stages of your report or sharing ideas in a two-way discussion with a friend.

Unit 11.2   Structuring the report

Your report must be structured in a way the reader finds logical, informative and coherent.

1 **As a quick revision of structure, briefly write definitions for or explanations of each of these key terms. Some of these may seem obvious, but it is useful to be completely clear about what each refers to.**

a   Title page: _____

b   Abstract: _____

c   Table of contents: _____

d   Introduction: _____

e   Hypothesis: _____

f   Methodology: _____

g   Perspectives: _____

h   Conclusion: _____

i   Recommendations: _____

j   Appendices: _____

2 **Read this extract from an introduction to a Cambridge Research Report. Which of the following aspects have been addressed in it? Underline and label each element.**

a   what is going to be examined or explored

b   results of a literature review

c   key concepts and/or perspectives

d   justification of the concepts and why they are relevant

e   hypothesis

> In this report, the question of the threat posed by cyber-warfare compared to conventional military force will be considered. It interrogates the term 'cyber-warfare', which is itself a contested concept, and looks at examples of so-called cyber-warfare perpetrated by a range of state actors such as the United States and Russia over the course of the last 10 years. It evaluates the effectiveness of such use in terms of destabilising perceived enemy states, and the impact on a range of areas from the economy to social and cultural fields. To explore the question, this report will investigate three areas: espionage; 'hard' and 'soft' threats; and the role of cyber-warfare in 'fake news', all of which will shed light on the extent to which cyber-warfare exists and its impact. It contends that cyber-warfare, far from being an imagined threat is both real and damaging in terms of its impact on democracy and the rule of law.

Key terms and language support

It is important that the paragraphs following your introduction sustain the same style, and also link logically. How effectively has this been done in the following paragraph?

> As I have suggested, the term 'cyber-warfare' is one that is open to debate. Whilst the motives of different states may be difficult to establish, their avowed purposes can be interrogated. Thus, if a particular state claims to be developing technology that allows them to track their own or other countries' citizens' actual or online actions, then it is reasonable to ask 'to what purpose?' At what point does responsible security cross the line into war against one's own people? Professor Adam Klinich of Trenton University, who specialises in cyber-warfare says in his article for *The Daily Universe*, 'Cyber-warfare is increasingly justified on the grounds of state security when evidence suggests it is in fact a cause of even greater security: when personal freedoms are invaded, the individual often turns against the state.' [1]
>
> Klinich's stance on cyber-warfare is well-known – he has published a number of critical reports about state-sponsored cyber-warfare – so it is important to explore alternative perspectives, and in the light of this essay, the extent to which these threats, if they exist, have local impact on us in our everyday lives. An alternative point of view is provided by...

Task 3

Answer these questions, using the pages at the back of the Workbook or a separate piece of paper.

a In what way does the first paragraph above refer back to content in the introduction? Which phrase tells the reader this?

b How does the second paragraph link to the previous one? Would it make sense if it came before the first? If so, why?

c In what way does the second paragraph seem to look forward?

d How are links made within each paragraph between points made and evidence or between one point and another? Can you identify particular words or phrases that help this 'linkage'?

e Is the academic style of the introduction maintained?

Reflection

Give a verbal introduction to a fellow student about your report, trying to cover the elements mentioned above and in the Student's Book. How effectively were you able to do it? If you struggled to explain, go back to your plans and check you are clear about what you intend to cover.

Unit 11.3 Writing the report

It is important to sustain an informed, academic style in your Cambridge Research Report, but one that is accessible to a non-specialist audience.

1 **What advice would you give a student starting the course with regard to the style you should use in the report? Create a simple checklist based on these issues, adding any guidance you have learned about, as shown in the example for terminology below.**

> Terminology: *Make sure the terms you use are relevant to your subject area / topic and are used consistently – and where specialist ones, explained for the reader.*
>
> Formality/informality: _____
>
> Signposting language: _____
>
> Clarity and concision: _____
>
> Idioms and colloquialisms: _____
>
> Vocabulary: _____
>
> Narrative versus analytic/critical writing: _____

2 **The following extract comes from a report that continues the theme of cyber-warfare as explored in Unit 11.2. It contains a number of faults.**

a Underline any stylistic issues that need addressing.

b Rewrite the extract, correcting anything you have identified (you may also need to add new text).

> One perspective we'll need to check out is related to 'Hacktivism', which has become a big deal in cyber-space. To call this 'warfare' may be a bit strong but it's enabled hackers to pursue their goals and make a massive impact on huge corporations and businesses which they object to. Think about a group like 'Anonymous'. Even as far back as 2008, their Project Chanology targeted the Church of Scientology. Clearly, this was not an attack on a nation state as such, there was no 'Cyber Pearl Harbor' here, but it demonstrated the impact a loosely-assembled collective could have on powerful bodies, and so leads to the question if they could do it, why not state-sponsored agencies?

_____
_____
_____
_____
_____
_____
_____
_____
_____
_____
_____

_____
_____
_____
_____
_____
_____
_____
_____
_____
_____
_____
_____
_____
_____
_____
_____
_____
_____
_____
_____

Key terms and language support

A number of terms with similar or even identical meanings often appear in academic essays or reports of this sort. Here are some potential groupings (some words are relevant to more than one category):

Argument	Process	Factor	Period	Concept
perspective	procedure	function	episode	principle
viewpoint	sequence	element	time	theory
opinion	structure	aspect	stage	method
interpretation	analysis	feature	phase	approach
version	progression	issue	point	model
reading	development	component	step	belief

Task 3

Review your own writing and identify words you have used that appear on these lists – or, if more informal, could be replaced with one.

Decide if the current word you use is 'fit for purpose'; is a 'perspective' the same as an 'interpretation'? Would 'principle' be better than 'approach' – or vice versa? Make sure you are clear about the most common meanings of these terms and apply them appropriately.

Reflection

Getting someone else to read your drafts regularly is a useful way to check that your writing is clear and designed for a non-specialist audience. If there is anything your reader doesn't understand – whether that's a term or a concept – make sure you have explained it clearly and concisely.

The written exam: Tables 1 and 2, and simple essay plan

Use the following grids/tables to practise your analysis and evaluation of evidence, arguments and perspectives in source texts you read as preparation for the written exam. You will find part-completed versions of these on pages 84 and 89 of the Student's Book.

Table 1: Strengths/weaknesses of evidence in an unseen text (you do not have to fill in both columns)

Factor to look for	Strength	Weakness
Status/reliability of authors, motive to be accurate		
Purpose or context of article		
Use of expert or official sources		
Range/balance of evidence		
Relevant or plausible evidence		
Use of statistics or data (vague or specific, relevant, etc.)		
Overall summary of strength of evidence		

Table 2: Identifying arguments in two documents

This is a simple grid for listing the key arguments made in two documents. Alternatively, jot your ideas directly into the essay plan.

Document 1	Document 2

Essay plan: Use this simple plan for structuring a response comparing the arguments in a practice exam-style question.

Introduction: A brief summary of the topic and the two documents	
Body of the essay Part 1: Arguments in Document 1	
Interim conclusion: Document 1	
Body of the essay Part 2: Arguments in Document 2	
Interim conclusion: Document 2	
Overall conclusion	

The Essay: Selecting issues, topics and questions

Use the following grids to support your development of ideas for the Essay at the start of the process. Feel free to adapt or develop your own tables or charts to reflect your way of working.

Template 1: Selecting a topic

Stages	Focus	Notes	Date due	Done?
1 Selecting a broad topic	Consider interests, news, further study			
2 Exploration	What does the topic mean to me?			
3 Development	Log ideas – what are my initial reactions? What do I need to research? Have I done a schema?			
4 Evaluation	Test the suitability of your topic. Is it a global issue? Does it engage different themes? Does it set up some form of argument/discussion?			
5 Narrowing the topic	Narrow the topic into issues that could engage a 'yes/no' discussion. Use schema to select areas of interest. What themes arise? Do themes lead to contrasting perspectives?			
Further actions needed?				

Template 2: Selecting a question

My final topic	Date due	Done?
My final chosen topic is: I chose this because:		

Selecting a question	Date due	Done?
My possible questions are: 1 2 3		

My final question	Date due	Done?
My final question is: I chose this because:		

Further actions needed?	

Research and referencing

The following simple grid is useful for recording where you have sourced material from. The rows are numbered here, for your own referencing.

Source and/ or title	Author	Date	URL or other location (e.g. publisher)	When accessed	Notes
1					
2					
3					
4					
5					
6					

Organising and developing research

Use this organisational chart to develop your ideas. First, write your question in the centre, then add further information to the outer hexagons. Look at page 112 of the Student's Book to help you.

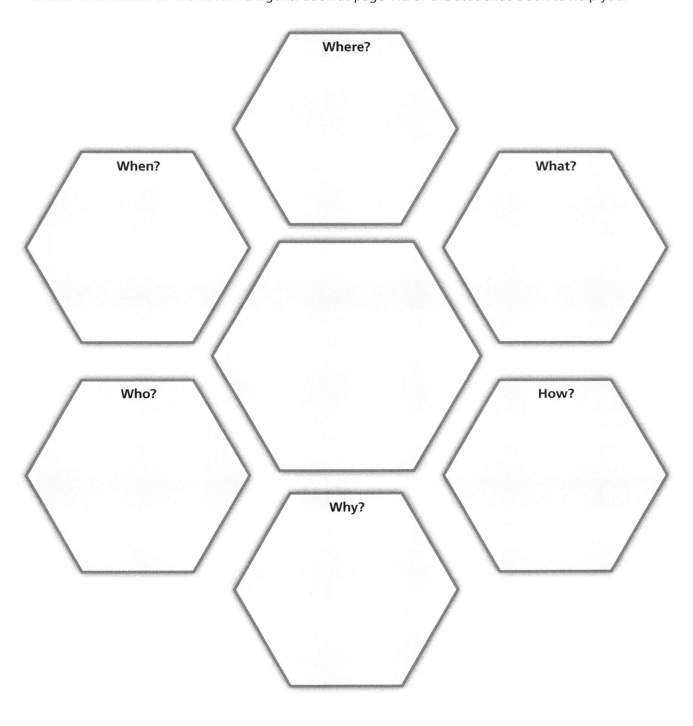

Where?

When?

What?

Who?

How?

Why?

Essay plan and structure

Use this template to check you have included the relevant content in your essay. You can adapt this structure, but try to cover all the elements in the table. Use the second column for any additional information or notes to yourself.

Introduction	Notes	Included?	More needed
Question (Y/N format)			
Catchy or engaging intro sentence			
Controversy			
Motivation			
My initial opinion			
Definitions			
Limitations			
Body of essay			
Perspective 1/Case study 1			
Perspective 2/Case study 2			
Perspective 3/Case study 3			
Synthesis of perspectives/ case studies			
Reflection on what has been learned/observed			
Conclusion			
Brief summary of evaluation of perspectives			
Reflective judgement on the question			
Change or confirmation of original view			
Limitations leading to suggestions for further research			
Answer			

Content editing

Use this grid to check your essay both as you write and once you have finished.

Overall structure	Done?	More needed?
Have I followed my plan (e.g. the right content for each section) – effective introduction; main body with its analysis of different perspectives, synthesis of ideas and evidence in arguments; reflections; a strong conclusion?		
Are new ideas in separate paragraphs?		
Do my paragraphs link logically and sequentially?		
Have I answered the questions posed?		

Style and expression	Done?	More needed?
Are my points clear?		
Is there support for all points made?		
Have points been supported with appropriate evidence and/or examples, and, where appropriate, sources quoted fluently?		
Have I used PEE (L) paragraph structures?		
Have I used signal words to indicate:		
• new ideas		
• evidence		
• conclusions?		

Proofreading	No	Comment
Are all my sentences complete (subject/verb/ capital letter/end punctuation)?		
Is my punctuation correct and are my sentences the correct length?		
Is my choice of vocabulary accurate?		
Is my use of pronouns clear?		
Have I used any jargon, slang or clichés which should be avoided?		
Have I spelled commonly confused words (there/ their) correctly?		
Are quotations introduced by a signal phrase?		
Are quotations accurately cited and referenced?		

The Team Project: Exploring potential ideas for your project

Stage 1: Use the following grid to note down ideas and help develop your own and your group's thinking.

Local problem

Potential local problem to explore	

Potential relevance and suitability

Aspects to consider	Notes
How was the issue important (or not) in the past?	
In what ways/how is it important now?	
What perspectives could be used to examine the issue?	
Who are the stakeholders involved? Who does the problem affect now and in the future?	
Where is the issue a problem?	
Who benefits or gains? Who loses as a result of this issue?	
Are there sufficient resources available? Where will you locate them?	
What 'live' (e.g. face to face) research might you have to do? Is this feasible?	
In what way is this globally relevant? Can you link the problem to one or more of the global topics in the syllabus? (e.g. changing identities, sport in an international context)	

Working as a team: Reflecting on your role and that of others
Key information

Who are the members of your team?
How are you communicating with them both within and outside class?
Do you have scheduled time slots to talk or meet? If so, when?
When is your next meeting/discussion? What do you have to do in order to be ready for it?

Your role

There are a number of roles individuals take on in teams (often more than one). For example, researcher, note-maker or recorder, debater, timekeeper, reporter, IT expert, language expert, energiser or harmoniser, strategy analyst, reflection coach. Which of these: are you taking on?   do you need to do more of?
Has your team allocated roles (not necessarily all of these)?   If not, when will this be done?
How confident do you feel about your team?   If there are issues you are concerned about, how will you resolve them?
How confident do you feel about your own role within the team?   If there are challenges for you, how will you resolve them?

Preparing for your presentation

For your research, you can either use the form/grid on page 57 of this Workbook, or create your own based on the one on page 136 of the Student's Book. However, to make sure you are on track to create your presentation, use this table.

Task/objective	Deadline	In progress? Complete?	Improvement needed?	Further action needed?
Identify, evaluate and select a variety of sources to research your local problem from a global perspective.				
Read and analyse texts (media and print-based) closely to identify any ideas of relevance.				
Make detailed notes to synthesise and summarise main points, possible arguments and evidence.				
Decide on and organise arguments. Select appropriate supporting evidence from your research and investigate further if needed.				
Decide on possible solutions to your problem. Discuss and compare the distinct perspectives.				
Present summary of individual perspectives on the team problem with arguments and solutions for peer feedback and review.				
Draft text of presentation slides.				

Draft presentation cue cards.				

Structuring your presentation

The following template is one possible way of structuring your presentation. Note that columns have been provided for you to reference any slides or cue cards you use (but don't feel you have to complete them). This has been 'stretched' over two pages to leave space for you to make notes.

Stage of presentation	Notes – key focus or content	Cue card(s)	Slide number(s)
Greeting/Welcome	Introducing local problem which is The rationale for my perspective which is		
Section 1a	Current situation/state of play which is		
Section 1b	My analysis and evaluation of key points		
Section 1c	The key arguments and evidence/examples		
Interim summary	Summing up key points so far		

Section 2a	Further points or perspectives to explore		
Section 2b	My analysis and evaluation of key points		
Section 2c	The key arguments and evidence/examples		
Interim summary	Summing up the second set of key points		
Solutions	Possible solutions or actions that could be taken Reasons/supporting evidence		
Conclusion	Summing up the problem as a whole and what needs to be done. Call to action?		

The Reflective Paper

The following grid is a lightly adapted version of the structure on page 160 of the Student's Book. You can use it to make basic notes but you may need to copy and write it out in order to add more detail.

Introduction to topic	
The problem I worked on	
Reflections on the effectiveness of teamwork	
My role and team roles What didn't go well and why What did go well and why	
Interim conclusion	
Suggested areas for improvement	
Reflections on the learning journey: knowledge	
What were my initial opinions and the impact of further research? What was the impact of other approaches within the team?	
Interim conclusion	
What was my learning journey? Where were my knowledge gaps?	
Reflection on the learning journey: skills	
How effective was my approach to research? Consider both strengths and weaknesses. What would I do next time to improve the research process?	
Was the form/style of my presentation engaging and clearly articulated? Having watched my presentation back, what would I do differently if I had to do it again? How logical and coherent were my arguments? In future, how would I better integrate my argument with the supporting visuals?	
Interim conclusion	
How effective was my presentation as a whole?	
Final conclusion	
What have I learned?	

The Cambridge Research Report: Report Action Plan

It is important you set yourself clear deadlines and timescales for preparing and writing the Cambridge Research Report. The grid below is one template you can use, or you can develop your own.

Activity	Timeline (timescale/dates for completion)	Completed?	Reflection or next action (if needed)

Activity bank (These are some of the tasks/actions you might add to the table above in the sequence that suits you – you may want to meet your teacher after each stage, or less frequently.)

- Research initial concept
- Research arguments/ perspectives for
- Conduct interviews
- Write index
- Redraft report
- Make further amendments

- Decide concept/title
- Research arguments/ perspectives against
- Check source referencing is correct
- Synthesise and reconstruct research

- Write first draft*
- Write abstract
- Meet teacher/supervisor
- Collate research
- Create writing plan
- Write proposal
- Proofread

Obviously the report itself will be divided into sections, so you might want to allocate specific time for each of these – e.g. the introduction.

Exploring methodologies

The approach you take to generating ideas for your report will be similar to the one you used for the Essay, but your final question will be narrower in scope and more academic, and is less likely to cut across themes. The key difference will be in the methodologies you use – some of which are very specific to one area (e.g. 'experimental' in sciences).

Jot down your title in the central box below.

Make notes in each of the outer boxes in terms of whether the methodology is useful or not, and give examples of what you might look at.

Empirical (measuring data in the 'real' world)	Quantitative data (able to be measured numerically)	Qualitative data (related to attitudes and opinions)
Experimental (controlled observations of things)	**YOUR TITLE**	Theoretical (making a hypothesis based on observations)
Interpretative (reading for different meanings, for example where one fixed meaning is unlikely)	Reading of signs, images and symbols	Close textual reading and analysis

Structuring your report

Use this basic two-page template for planning the contents of your report. Notes or bullet points should go in the right-hand boxes.

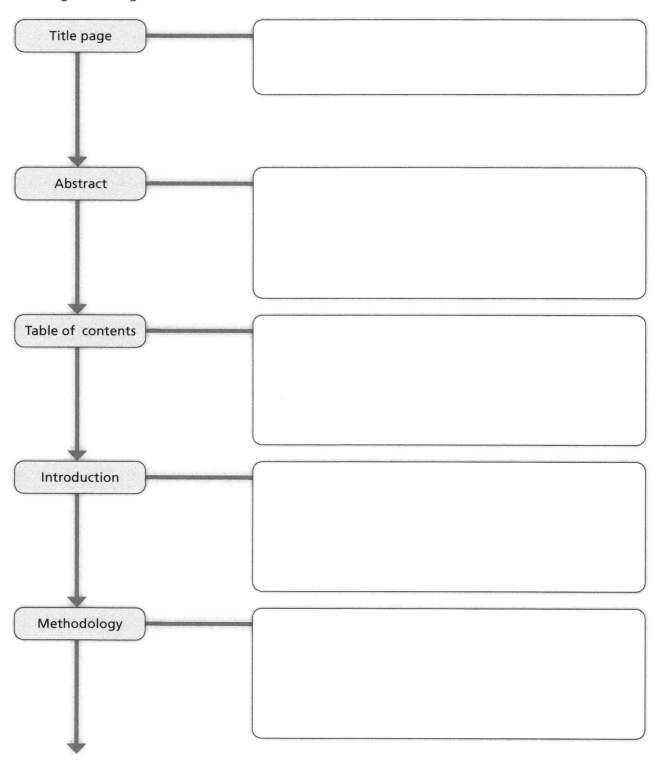

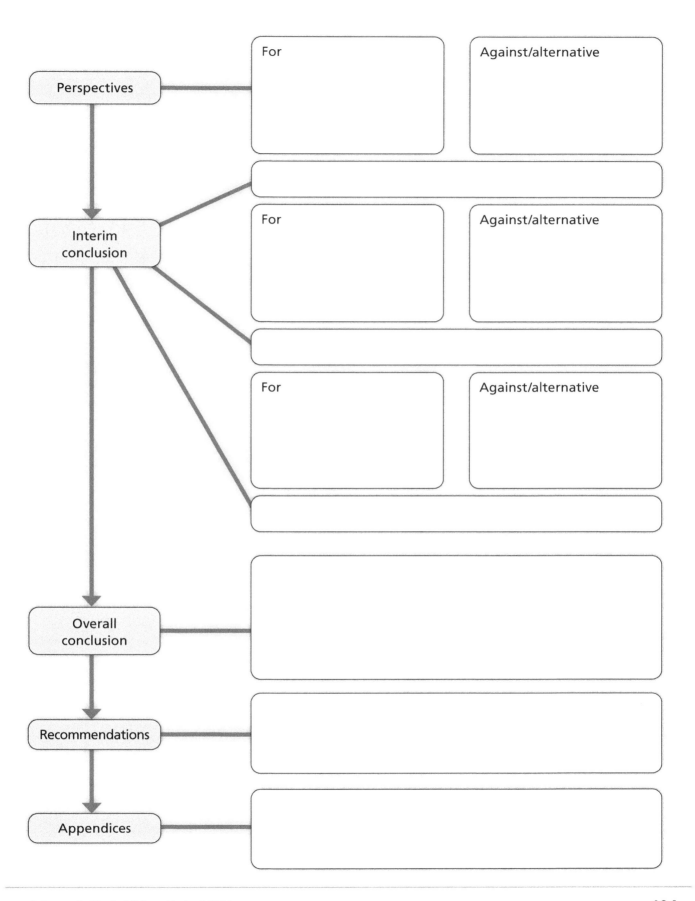

Perspectives

For

Against/alternative

Interim conclusion

For

Against/alternative

For

Against/alternative

Overall conclusion

Recommendations

Appendices

Drafting your report

Use the following pages to start drafting your report from the Introduction onwards. As a way of reflecting on your style and content, either as you progress or after you finish this opening part, you could label your own work with the following features:

(AW) Analytic writing (PW) Persuasive writing (C/D) Critical/discursive writing (SS) Subject-specific term   (AV) Academic vocabulary (SL) Signposting language   (SE) Source/evidence

Notes